PERFECTLY HEDGED

Interested in learning more?
In-person and online training available.
Visit our website for additional information.

Join the Perfectly Hedged community!
Follow us on LinkedIn for new insights,
updates and exclusive offers.

Let's connect, I'd love to hear from you:

SAMUEL BASI
Founder & Author
Perfectly Hedged LLC

+1 203-391-8021
samuel.basi@perfectlyhedged.com
www.perfectlyhedged.com
linkedin.com/company/perfectly-hedged-llc

For rights and permissions, please contact the following:

Samuel.Basi@perfectlyhedged.com

About the Author

After graduating with a bachelor's degree (with honors) in economics from the University of Loughborough, United Kingdom, Samuel Basi embarked on a successful career in the commodities industry.

Samuel began his career at Trafigura, one of the world's largest commodity trading houses. He has worked in the industry for the past seventeen years across multiple commodities, desks, and continents.

His career has taken him from Switzerland to the United States, with roles spanning operations, the deals desk, physical trading, and derivatives trading. This breadth of experience has given him a comprehensive understanding of how commodity markets function in the real world, beyond theory and textbooks.

Samuel is the founder of Perfectly Hedged LLC, a leading education and consultancy firm that helps companies across the commodity supply chain improve market understanding, reduce costly errors, and increase profitability.

He is also the author of *Perfectly Hedged: A Practical Guide To Base Metals*, a widely used industry reference for risk management and hedging in physical markets.

Drawing on his broad exposure to the global commodity trading ecosystem, Samuel wrote this book to demystify an industry that remains opaque - often by design - and to provide readers with a clear, practical framework for understanding how physical commodity markets truly operate.

Table Of Contents

1. Introduction

When you hear the word *commodity,* you probably think about the latest price for crude oil or copper flashing across a CNBC or Bloomberg news ticker. But physical commodities are far more than numbers on a screen.

Commodities are the bedrock of communities around the world. They have been critical resources since humans have existed. From primitive bartering of agricultural products such as livestock and grain to today's intricate trade of oil and metal products. Commodities fuel our ability to travel, manufacture goods, and build machinery that continues to advance society.

But what exactly is a commodity, and why is the industry seeing an explosion of interest in recent years?

Every day begins with commodities whether you realize it or not. Your morning cup of coffee comes from beans grown on a coffee farm in Brazil. The smart phones we can't live without require refined and precious metals to function. The cars we drive to work are made from steel sheet and powered by gasoline. All of these items are the products of countless workers, thousands of miles of transport, and layers of financing.

But to the end user, these details are often invisible, and it is this hidden complexity that makes the commodities industry so hard to understand from the outside, yet so fascinating to those who work within it.

Commodities differ from finished consumer goods because they are standardized and, to a large extent, interchangeable. A barrel of crude oil that meets a certain specification is the same whether it comes from Nigeria, Saudi Arabia, or the United States. The same is true for bushels of wheat, ingots of aluminum, or drums of frozen concentrated orange juice. This homogeneity allows commodities to be traded globally, often traveling thousands of miles between each stage of processing.

There are of course nuances in the production of every commodity. Commodities are not always identical and different consumers may require different specifications even within the same product. For example, oil refineries must plan which blends to buy depending on seasonal requirements. These subtle differences are often where traders find opportunities to exploit.

Broadly speaking, commodities can be divided into two main categories - hard and soft - each with its own dynamics and risks.

Hard commodities are natural resources extracted or mined from the earth. They include energy products such as crude oil, natural gas, and coal; base metals such as iron ore, copper, and aluminum; and precious metals such as gold and silver. Hard commodities can often be stored for long periods without deterioration. Their demand cycles tend to be cyclical, and bringing new supply projects online can take decades, making supply slow to adjust to demand.

Soft commodities are grown rather than mined. They include products such as wheat, corn, coffee, and cotton as well as livestock such as cattle or hogs. These commodities are far more exposed to seasonality, weather, disease, and fungus than hard commodities. Transporting and storing soft commodities requires stricter environmental controls to protect quality. Many soft commodities must be transported or stored in temperature-controlled facilities to prevent degradation. Prices can experience sharp swings due to environmental factors such as droughts, pests, and harvest cycles. These factors can alter global supply in a single season.

The two categories are however becoming increasingly linked. There is now substantial crossover between agricultural products and energy trading for biofuel. Corn is fermented to create ethanol which is further blended with gasoline, particularly in the United States. Sugarcane is also used to create ethanol in Brazil. Soybeans are the leading vegetable oil used in biodiesel production in the United States. Palm oil is the major biodiesel feedstock in Southeast Asia. As a result, the prices of these agricultural products are increasingly correlated with biofuel demand.

The surge of interest in commodities in recent years is not accidental. Geopolitics, supply chain shocks, and the global energy transition have thrust commodities into the spotlight. Once viewed in certain regions as a niche part of global trade, commodities are now being recognized as what they truly are: essential components of daily life with micro and macro implications on a global scale.

For anyone seeking to understand how economies function, or aiming to build a career in this industry, gaining a solid understanding of commodities is a requirement. As governments race to secure long-term access to critical commodities through investment, protectionism, or trade agreements, historical trade flows are shifting. Understanding how commodities are produced, transported, and traded is essential not only for navigating today's markets, but also for anticipating the future of global trade.

A Personal Touch

A common theme throughout this book is the importance of relationships and the human element in commodity trading. Trading is not simply numbers on a screen and words in a contract; it is the stories behind face-to-face meetings that allow traders to build global books and long-term success.

With that in mind, between each chapter of this book you will find a personal story from my career in trading. For obvious reasons, I have anonymized some of the names, but the events themselves are true.

Physical commodity trading places you in front of people and in situations that are unfamiliar and, to the average person, occasionally unbelievable. I hope these stories offer a glimpse into some of the lesser-told aspects of commodity trading: the moments you won't see in financial statements.

Some stories come with lessons; others might just put a smile on your face. But I hope all of them deepen your passion for the industry.

If you are reading this book, you are likely to have more than a passing interest in commodities. Many of you are looking to build a career in the field. Maybe one day you will have as many stories to share as I do, and perhaps even better ones.

2. Why Do Commodity Traders Exist?

Commodity trading exists across every commodity category. Whether that's metals, energy products, or agricultural commodities, each commodity and the traders who trade it play a vital role in global trade.

Commodity traders have a long and storied history. Even the earliest civilizations have been recorded trading commodities. In Mesopotamia, the Sumerians used clay tokens to represent the quantities of a commodity, such as grain or goats, to be delivered. Ancient Greeks and Romans traded gold, silver, spices, and cloth.

Long before modern commodity exchanges, trading firms dealt goods such as sugar, tobacco, and coffee during the Age of Exploration. As European explorers sailed to the Americas, Africa, and Asia, they established companies such as the Virginia Company, the Dutch East India Company, and the British East India Company. These companies were a precursor to modern stock corporations that allowed ordinary people to invest in their expeditions by buying shares in the company. Investors shared in both the potential profits and the risk of loss during voyages, helping finance the expeditions.

Some of these early exploration companies like the Dutch East India Company grew so large that they maintained their own naval forces to protect their trade routes. At its peak, its fleet included 150 merchant ships and forty warships - crucial to safeguarding the company's economic interests and expanding territorial control.

Physical trading of commodities involves transporting goods from the point of production through to the place of consumption. To a large extent physical trading is similar across the entire commodity complex. While each commodity has its nuances, a lot of the fundamentals remain similar across different supply chains.

Historically, the reason commodity traders existed was straightforward: Very few people or companies had access to producers, consumers, and the trade routes connecting them. Producers of commodities rarely had links to consumers beyond their areas of production. Traders served as essential intermediaries who connected production with consumption.

But in today's global economy, where producers often have direct access to end consumers, the question arises: Why do traders exist? What value do traders add? What makes a producer sell to a trader instead of directly to the consumer or a consumer buy from a trader rather than from a producer?

The answer lies in the missing links of the commodity trading life cycle. Traders complete those links and provide a valuable service to both ends of the supply chain. If there is a way to extract value, traders will find it.

<u>Financing</u>

A primary reason traders exist today is related to how commodities are financed. Producers prefer to receive payment for their production as quickly as possible after producing it. Producers may even request payment in advance of producing a commodity.

In contrast, consumers want to pay for goods as many days as possible after taking delivery. Payment terms of net thirty days after receipt of goods are common, but terms of anything up to 360 days after receipt are not unheard of.

Most of the time, producers cannot accommodate consumers' preference for paying on extended terms because it delays cash flow and poses counterparty risk. If the consumer defaults before paying for the goods, the producer will suffer a significant loss. Producers prefer keeping cash on hand for capital expenditure rather than tying it up with consumers.

Consumers meanwhile want to minimize the time period between paying for their inputs and creating receivables for their finished goods.

Traders bridge this gap by leveraging their banking relationships and substantial financing capability to facilitate both sides of the trade. By offering producers prompt payment and being willing to extend credit terms to consumers, they create value for both ends of the chain. Traders may also be willing to pay to insure sales contracts, mitigating the counterparty credit exposure that producers are not willing to take on.

This is far from simple. Traders employ entire departments and deploy significant human capital dedicated to financing. These teams develop traditional and non-traditional funding methods, increasing their ability to offer creative solutions to producers and consumers alike. These efforts often make trade finance lines at trading houses cheaper than the internal borrowing costs for producers and consumers.

Relationships

Relationships remain a critical pillar of commodity trading. In an era where face-to-face interaction is declining, commodity trading continues to buck the trend. Traders that fail to develop relationships on both sides of the supply chain will not survive in the long term.

Traders spend years cultivating relationships with producers and consumers worldwide. The comfort, reliability, and trust built over time create a natural barrier to entry for new participants. Proven, reliable performance by traders over years in successfully executing business continues to give traders an edge.

Producers and consumers often lack the time and resources to build the global networks that traders maintain. By working with traders, they benefit from the extensive links traders have established, effectively diversifying their networks.

Market Making

Traders are often described as market-makers because they provide continuous liquidity and price discovery. But their role extends far beyond matching bids and offers. Unlike derivative markets, physical commodity markets lack a central clearing house that guarantees settlement. There is no institution standing behind each side of the trade. Instead, traders assume that role.

Producers want certainty of sales, often on a predictable schedule. Consumers want certainty of supply, often with flexible delivery. A trader will buy from a producer even without a downstream consumer secured and sell to consumers without having procured the material. In doing so, they absorb these mismatches in timing, location, specification, and credit.

Traders guarantee flow by absorbing the risks and uncertainties that neither side of the supply chain wants to bear or can handle. A refinery can run consistently knowing the trader will deliver. A mine can operate knowing a trader will take the material regardless of short-term market conditions.

In this sense, traders perform a quasi-clearing function. They are not clearing houses in the legal or exchange sense, but they do stand in the middle of the trade and guarantee performance to both sides. Traders smooth both the physical and financial logistics between supply and demand. In the futures markets, clearing houses do this through margin requirements and daily settlements. In physical markets, traders do this through their balance sheets, logistics networks, risk-management frameworks, and global relationships.

Offtake and Sole-Supplier Agreements

Financing arrangements are linked to offtake agreements, though not always. To secure long-term supply, traders may finance a project for a producer in exchange for a multi-year contract granting them a percentage (or all) of the production linked to that project. Accessing capital for new supply projects has become challenging as banks impose stricter collateral requirements.

Traders can provide relatively inexpensive capital and in return secure multi-year supply. Producers gain a guaranteed buyer for their production and traders expand their market footprint.

Traders may also offer fixed terms to a producer that a consumer would not offer on multi-year deals. Traders are happy to take a long-term view of the market, allowing them to be more aggressive in contract negotiations.

Similarly, traders may also offer consumers multi-year contracts, including sole-supplier agreements committing to cover 100 percent of the consumption requirements. For consumers planning expansion, a guaranteed supply is invaluable. Traders, sourcing from multiple origins, can provide security that single-site producers cannot.

Geographical Arbitrage

Another reason traders exist is geographical arbitrage. Arbitrage is not only a paper trading term. Physical traders exploit price differences for the same commodity in different geographical regions.

Physical traders often have a presence in multiple global locations with major offices in the biggest trading hubs. In contrast, producers and consumers are often located in only one market. This imbalance presents an opportunity for traders to expand the supply network and create tangible value.

By selling to a trader, a producer expands their global reach. The trader can ship commodities to whichever location offers the best return. Traders are far less dependent on local markets to be performing at any given time.

Similarly, a consumer buying from a trader gains immediate access to the global supply chain rather than relying solely on local production. Buying from traders allows them to receive production from a much larger and diverse number of production points.

Timing

Timing plays a crucial role in commodity trading. The production and consumption of commodities can be extremely fluid in nature. While every producer is aiming for consistency, many factors can disrupt or alter production rates including:

- Weather events: hurricanes, droughts, floods, extreme cold
- Operational issues: equipment failures, maintenance downtime, unplanned outages
- Labor disruptions: strikes, shortages, safety shutdowns
- Regulatory changes: environmental restrictions, new standards
- Logistics constraints: port congestion, transport delays, freight bottlenecks
- Geopolitical risks: sanctions, conflict, political instability

Traders have a unique ability to adapt quickly to changing supply and demand conditions that producers and consumers cannot.

Consumers operate on strict delivery schedules tied to their own production cycles. They may need specific volumes at certain times of the month, sometimes spaced out evenly, sometimes more sporadically. They may have different volume requirements at different times of the year based on changing seasonal consumption rates. Demand can fluctuate suddenly in both directions and traders can adjust deliveries to meet consumers' exact requirements.

Likewise, production schedules for producers can be evenly spread throughout the month or year, or it can vary based on seasonality. Producers can also experience periods of maintenance (planned or unplanned) that affect production rates.

For producers and consumers to match up their schedules in a way that suits both their needs can be extremely difficult. Traders can store material, sometimes for extended periods of time, offering producers and consumers greater flexibility than they would otherwise have.

Speed is another key advantage. While onboarding a new customer may take weeks or even months at most traditional companies, traders can often complete due-diligence checks within twenty-four to forty-eight hours. This allows them to act on opportunities far faster than producers or consumers can.

Logistics Expertise

Traders have spent decades perfecting their structures to become experts in logistics. Their teams have specialized knowledge that enables them to handle the transport of commodities across the globe, be it inland or overseas. This often requires multiple modes of transport such as rail, truck, barge, vessel, or pipeline.

Just as traders invest significant effort in developing relationships with producers and consumers, their operations and scheduling departments spend years building relationships with freight companies, forwarders, and brokers to secure access to global trade routes.

Even with this specialized knowledge, transporting hundreds of thousands of tons of material across the globe is difficult. Producers and consumers excel in their own fields, but they often lack the personnel and operational infrastructure needed to handle the same volume of transportation. Traders are willing to accept the high overhead costs of professionally staffing their desks with employees who can guarantee reliable delivery of commodities.

Many traders transport commodities in much higher volumes than any single producer or consumer. This allows traders to leverage economies of scale to lower their logistics costs in ways producers and consumers cannot.

For both producers and consumers, the ability to transfer all costs and the significant risks that come with physically transporting goods to traders is often worth paying a premium for.

This is not the case for all producers and consumers, of course. Some believe that handling the commodity transport themselves will save money in the long term, and when done correctly it can certainly do so. But many producers and consumers prefer to save themselves the cost and effort by relying on the traders' expertise to ensure material is picked up at the point of production, and delivered to the point of consumption.

Diversification

Diversification is a key reason traders exist. When a consumer buys a commodity directly from a producer, they accept the supply risk. If an event prevents the producer from delivering, the consumer must rebuy the material from the market at that time and at whatever the new market price is. While force majeure events are rare, they do happen, and consumers do not want to find themselves at the risk of shutting down their business because they cannot access supply. Or paying significantly more because the market has tightened since their original contract with the producer.

When buying from a trader, a consumer is not tied to a single supplier. Traders are obliged to use their global connections to fulfil a consumer contract from a different source, regardless of disruption at a single site.

Similarly, when producers sell directly to consumers, they bear the risk that buyers will renege on the deal. If that occurs, the producer will have to sell that excess material at prevailing market levels - often at a loss - or finance the unsold material for an unknown period. Consistent, reliable payment is key to producers. By selling to a trader, the producer avoids the risk of disruption to a consumer.

Traders have multiple counterparties on both the supply and demand sides of the trade. While they are not immune to defaults, traders face far fewer supply and consumption risks than producers and consumers face daily.

Hedging

Producers and consumers often execute their hedging strategies through traders. Producers want to fix prices when they are high, whereas consumers want to fix prices when they are low. When a producer directly faces a consumer, they have different hedging goals.

Traders bridge this gap by allowing each side to fix prices at the moment that best suits their individual exposure. This can eliminate the need for producers and consumers to set up their own hedging desks, which can be costly and require specialist knowledge and systems to manage.

Chapter Summary

- For as long as people have been producing and consuming commodities, there have been traders adding value in the middle of those operations.
- Traders play a necessary and important role in the global trade of commodities.
- Traders provide much-needed liquidity to markets, drastically increasing efficiency. If producers had to deal exclusively with end consumers, and vice versa, the global supply chain would face increased risks and likely increased costs.
- Traders create value for both ends of the supply chain by utilizing their relationships, financing capabilities, long-term commitments, geographical presence, expertise, and creativity.
- Given the benefits that traders bring, their presence in the market is unlikely to diminish.

First Time on a Private Jet

"Act like you've been there before" is a phrase that can be applied to various walks of life, but it's particularly true in commodity trading. Composure matters; you never want to come across as inexperienced in a negotiation. The best traders carry a certain level of confidence and self-belief that prevents them from second-guessing themselves, even when they are improvising.

So when I was told that the CEO was coming to the US office to visit our biggest clients, I was excited that our mode of transport would be the company jet - though I had to keep reminding myself to act like it wasn't my first time.

Flying privately is more involved than I realized. I had figured that you could turn up at your plane and instruct the pilot to take you to your preferred destination. Instead, detailed flight plans need to be submitted, so the team got to work planning the most efficient routes to see our various clients.

On the day of the flight we headed to a relatively small airport. One of the benefits of a business jet is that it does not require the same runway length as commercial planes, so it can fly from pretty much anywhere. As we walked to the plane I fought the urge to take out my phone to take pictures. This is just another flight, I kept telling myself. That said, the bathroom on board was nicer than the one in my house at the time, so I did sneak a photo of that.

Ironically, for a job that involves near-constant travel, I have never been a great flyer. Flying usually involves alcohol to calm me down. But considering I was sitting opposite the global head of metals trading and the CEO, I stuck to water. I immediately regretted that choice on takeoff.

I quickly found that the takeoff angle for these jets is far steeper than I am used to. While everyone else casually grabbed their laptops and started working as if g-forces didn't apply to them, I gripped the arm rests so tightly that they probably still show my fingerprints. Between saying my last goodbyes to my loved ones in my head, I shot a quick glance over at the CEO, who was chuckling to himself.

“First time in a private jet?” he asked me.

So much for acting as if I’d been there. I nodded nervously back.

“Don’t worry, you get used to the takeoffs. Drink?”

Another nod.

“Great, beers coming up…actually, perhaps we should get you something stronger.”

3. Roles In Commodity Trading

For those of you looking to embark on a career in the commodities industry, there are many different paths you can take. While trading is often the most common aspiration for new joiners, commodity trading encompasses a wide variety of roles, all working together to create value in the global supply chain. Commodity companies are not simply a group of traders making deals. Behind each contract are dozens of employees, from front to middle to back office, who facilitate smooth transactions.

Understanding the desk that you are targeting or happen to be working on, and how other desks connect to it will add tangible value to your career. For those less familiar with the industry, this chapter will also provide you with insight into the work each department does, helping you identify which roles might be the best fit for your skills, interests, and long-term goals.

Accounting

The accounting department tracks and reconciles invoices, payments, and other revenue streams at a trading firm. It will be heavily involved in the liquidation of contracts, ensuring that what is being reported in the mark-to-market and profits and losses (P&Ls) is accurate compared to the actual inflows and outflows of revenue.

Accounting will also ensure that all trading activities are reported sufficiently to meet audit and tax requirements. At public companies, accounting departments will prepare consolidated financial statements and liaise with external auditors. This ensures figures comply with the reporting standards set by the listing exchange. This requires a highly disciplined approach to guarantee accounts are closed within the required timelines.

Private companies do not face the same regulatory reporting requirements; however they will still report semiannually or annually to lenders to maintain credit facilities and covenants, and good relationships with tax authorities. Accounting departments will prepare balance sheets, but the level of disclosure may be less detailed than public filings. Some privately held companies will voluntarily issue audited annual reports to provide transparency to banks and counterparties.

Depending on the reporting a company follows, the accounting department will be heavily involved in monitoring the value of inventories, hedges, derivative positions, and physical contracts to ensure that correct valuations are used to report the company's performance.

Accounting departments work closely with treasury and finance departments as well as with middle-office functions.

Treasury

The treasury department directly manages the liquidity and ability of companies to make payments and settle trades. It typically handles any foreign exchange component of trades, ensuring that cash is available and that the company has access to the correct currency.

The treasury department will process incoming and outgoing transactions and manage the company's cash flow. It will work with the middle-office on matters such as future payments and receivables to support cash-flow planning.

Ensuring the company has the liquidity to make payments is why trading companies set payment cutoffs. Payments usually must be advised at least one business day in advance of the requested payment date to allow sufficient time to line up cash. Same-day payments (requests to pay the invoices the same day they are received) can strain bank lines and are therefore the exception, not the rule.

The treasury department will also handle any margin call payments on hedges related to initial and variation margin limits. The timely payment of any margin call is vital to the company's ability to continue to execute hedges. Given how volatile commodity prices can be, planning around margin payments requires constant monitoring, particularly at large trading firms with significant derivative positions tied to their hedging procedures.

Finance

While the treasury department handles the physical flow of money in and out of a company, the finance department is integral in ensuring the company has access to sufficient, well-priced funding. Without adequate lines of credit, trading companies would grind to a halt. Trading companies face near-constant pressure to expand financing lines to support increased trade volume and the volatility of commodity prices.

When we talk about hedging, we say companies hedge to make themselves price-agnostic. But this doesn't mean companies that hedge no longer care about commodity prices. Just ask the finance department whether it would prefer copper at $10,000/mt or $8,000/mt, or crude oil at $70/barrel versus $100/barrel. The finance department cares deeply about price levels because lower prices free up credit capacity, whereas higher prices quickly consume it.

The finance department maintains and develops banking relationships to manage both short and long-term funding for the trading activities. This can range from managing revolving credit facilities and repo transactions, to arranging larger structured financing such as bond issuances and securitizations.

The finance department works hand in hand with the company's commercial arms, and as such it walks the line between middle and back-office. It is often involved early in deal negotiations, providing solutions for major purchases.

Most payments will be overseen or approved by the finance department before passing to treasury to ensure compliance with the terms of the physical contract and to avoid issues with the financing bank. Specialists from the finance team carefully review letters of credit to prevent document errors because minor inaccuracies can result in costly delays.

The finance team also monitors documents as material moves throughout the supply chain to ensure title passes correctly and at the appropriate time and that material moves only when it is authorized.

Credit

The credit department will assess the financial performance and health of potential and existing counterparties with whom traders engage.

It will be involved during onboarding new counterparties and typically require financial statements to determine whether credit terms can be extended for a physical sale, or if a trader would be prepared to pay a supplier before taking delivery of the material.

The credit department works with commercial teams to provide language for contracts that reduce a trader's risk when offering terms to a counterparty. Contracts are typically written so credit can be withdrawn if a counterparty's financial conditions deteriorate, or simply at the trader's discretion. Credit departments continually monitor credit terms and company exposures to ensure a trader's risks do not exceed agreed limits.

A single default can seriously affect an entire trading desk's annual profits. For this reason the credit team also works with external insurance companies to protect firms against nonpayment or default. Deals can be credit insured individually, usually reserved for larger volume contracts, or firms can obtain broad credit coverage that covers all contracts with extended credit terms. Trading companies must adhere to the limits and stipulations of credit insurance companies to ensure reimbursement should it be required.

Compliance

The compliance department ensures that all procedures designed to mitigate financial, legal, and reputational risks are being followed.

Trading firms are under near-constant scrutiny from lenders, stakeholders, and global regulators. They need to be able to prove their employees are following strict guidelines regarding all applicable laws.

Compliance takes a leading role in crafting internal training for employees to demonstrate that the company has taken a proactive approach to preventing staff from breaching laws or regulations.

The fines that can be levied upon trading firms for breaching these laws can be devastating. In recent years, bribery cases in the commodities sector have led to penalties of hundreds of millions of dollars, imposed by regulators in the United States, Switzerland, and the United Kingdom.

Given the global nature of commodity trading, members of the compliance team must have broad knowledge of not only local markets but also international standards. As these laws evolve, companies must continually adapt to reflect the most updated requirements including new controls on anti-bribery, sanctions screening, and revised environmental, social, and governance (ESG) policies.

Compliance not only prevents regulatory breaches but also gives the company the confidence to operate at full potential in any geography.

Analysts

In recent years, firms of all sizes have brought their analysis in-house. Although they may still consult the larger research agencies to supplement their own work, analysts at trading companies are producing their own bespoke research.

Analysts work closely with front-office teams, building models that provide the traders with information they can use to help craft trading strategies. This ranges from simple supply-and-demand curves and production and consumption data to larger macroeconomic modeling, geopolitical analysis, and regulatory developments.

Physical trading houses utilize an increasing amount of coding so if you are interested in this quantitative field, coding skills are increasingly a differentiator for analysts in trading houses.

Analysis can be customer, product, or region-specific, or have broader book or company-level implications.

While analysts have always been part of derivative trading strategies, they are now a central part of the physical trading ecosystem offering real-time insights to traders and risk teams.

Skilled analysts understand not only the data but also the trader's commercial language. They provide the right data at the right moment, positively influencing profits.

<u>Operations</u>

Operations roles span the broad spectrum of the commodity lifecycle and are among the most critical middle-office functions at a trading firm. Once the front-office has made a commercial decision, operations is responsible for executing all physical aspects of the trade. It will arrange all logistics to transport products from point A to point B and sometimes C, D, E, F, and G. It ensures that the physical movement of the material aligns with producers' and consumers' expectations.

Although the exact role of an operator can vary by company, and titles may differ, the overall responsibilities are very similar.

Operators work with practically every other department daily. They will arrange payments and work with the finance and treasury departments to ensure documents are prepared in accordance with contracts. They engage with risk teams to ensure correct hedging of physical contracts. They are often responsible for allocating the costs to contracts, checking mark-to-markets and P&Ls before accounting liquidates those contracts.

Operators usually sit directly with their front-office teams to enable real-time communication regarding physical trades. Operations are often the first to learn about changes to shipping schedules and frequently receive requests from counterparties. The ability to relay this information immediately to the front-office, finance, and risk departments facilitates quick and informed decision-making that can directly influence a deal's profitability.

Externally, operations teams negotiate logistics and storage rates. This process requires them to build relationships with service providers because logistics costs are often the largest contributor to profit or loss on a physical contract.

Operators also need to develop relationships with suppliers and consumers to maintain excellent information flow - not only regarding deliveries but also regarding opportunities for additional profits. Operators are not simply there to move material. By understanding market prices and conditions, and how their impact on physical contracts, operators can add tangible.

Scheduler

In energy trading, the operator role is typically referred to as a scheduler.

Schedulers are also responsible for the physical movement of energy products, but a key difference is that pipelines are a method of transporting the commodity. Schedulers are deeply involved in pipeline and vessel scheduling, which can be more complex than other commodities due to the nature of liquid cargoes. They also encounter demurrage claims and blending operations more frequently than their counterparts in metals and dry bulk.

Similar to operations teams, schedulers are also responsible for implementing the terms of the physical contracts. Volumes, quality, timing - schedulers arrange all of these.

Schedulers oversee the accuracy of shipping documentation and other crucial documents. They monitor stock levels and work hand-in-hand with the front office and risk teams to ensure physical contracts are executed correctly. They also coordinate with the risk, finance, and accounting departments to ensure precise hedging, payment processing, and reporting.

By managing logistics, costs, and documents, schedulers directly influence the profitability of energy trades.

Risk

The risk desk is responsible for mitigating a company's exposure to price volatility. Often referred to as the hedge desk or deals desk, the risk department works closely with front and middle-office teams to ensure the company is protected against price fluctuations in the commodities they trade. Risk teams will execute derivative trades to hedge these risks for the physical desks.

This includes both outright price risk, foreign exchange risk, spread risk, cross-exchange risk (arbitrage), and any other hedgeable exposures. Although some firms do take speculative risks, this is typically performed outside of the physical contracts. Risk teams will ensure that physical trading books remain within the accepted limits designated by management at all times.

Some physical traders will aim to achieve a perfect hedge - whereby they mitigate *all* price risk related to their physical contracts. Even small exposures can cause catastrophic losses if not quickly identified and addressed. When I was on a hedge desk, no one was allowed to go home until we had confirmed every trading book was square and all price risk had been mitigated.

Risk teams need deep expertise in the derivative markets they trade on. They also need to develop relationships with the brokers they execute through. At some trading firms this may be an internal derivative desk, at other firms this will be directly with the exchange brokers themselves.

Traders

Traders, or front-office teams are the primary revenue generators for a trading company. Physical traders will negotiate and execute contracts, attempting to create value for both ends of the supply chain, while also creating a profit for the trading company.

Although there are many ways to create profits, the backbone of any physical trading company is the ability for traders to use geographical, informational, and situational arbitrage to position the trader between producers and consumers. From very short-term spot opportunities, to multi-year contracts, traders are buying and selling commodities and establishing relationships across all parts of the supply chain.

Physical traders will spend extensive time traveling to meet their counterparties and build their relationships with them. If you aspire to become a physical trader, you should get accustomed to traveling!

Physical traders work closely with operations, risk, finance, legal, credit, and compliance to ensure trades are well executed and remain within established company guidelines and limits.

Physical trading companies will often have dedicated derivative traders working alongside the physical teams. Derivative traders will devise strategies that use short and long-term positioning when they believe they have an edge in the market.

This could be from a fundamental trading standpoint, a technical trading standpoint, or a mixture of both. They utilize futures, forwards, options, swaps, and other derivative instruments to generate profits. They commonly work closely with the physical trading teams and analysts to help formulate their views.

Derivative traders operate under strict limits that define the maximum loss, commonly known as value at risk (VaR).

Business Development

While traders typically focus on their own specific trading books, business development teams cover a wide variety of products. They may focus on larger, longer-term, and more wide-ranging projects that will add value to the entire organization.

Projects are not always front-office facing. Though this desk works closely with the front-office, it often focuses on ideas that support the middle and back-office teams, as well as group infrastructure and systems development.

Business development works closely with most departments including IT and systems, human resources (HR), and management to help advance the company's overall corporate vision.

Mergers and Acquisitions

Driven by the green energy transition and the globalization of the commodity trading world, mergers and acquisitions (M&A) departments are becoming crucial to larger and midsize traders.

Assets, and the guaranteed offtake they provide, are central to expanding a trader's footprint in the market. As margins come under pressure, securing and growing trading volumes has become essential. Ownership, or holding a stake in assets such as mines, smelters, refineries, infrastructure, ports, or storage locations, is now a core focus for many trading companies.

M&A teams work closely with front office, finance, and management to deploy company capital in ways that advance trading ambitions.

Systems and IT

Traders can only operate within their systems' limits. For this reason, firms invest heavily in bespoke trading software that facilitates seamless information flow across departments allowing for efficient execution of contracts.

Providing traders, as well as middle-office, and back-office employees with timely information is crucial to longevity in this business. Timely information prevents mistakes and enables accurate commercial decisions. The commodities industry is extremely fast-paced and the ability to act quickly is vital.

Trading companies also have to manage their IT security carefully. Scams and security attacks are a constant threat, particularly when transaction amounts are billions of dollars. Ensuring that systems remain secure is an ongoing undertaking for the IT department.

Legal

Whether managed in-house or by external teams, the legal department is critical to any trading firm. From overseeing the physical contracts that accompany every deal and crafting terms and conditions that protect traders to dealing with the threat of legal action, lawyers are intimately involved in trading decisions.

The legal department works closely with compliance to ensure that actions taken by members of all departments comply not only with the law but also with the company guidelines.

Given the breadth of commodities, products, and jurisdictions involved, trading firms often rely on specialized legal teams organized by commodity or region to ensure comprehensive coverage.

Human Resources

Human resources (HR) departments play a multifaceted role in a trading company. They handle a multitude of internal processes and also onboard new employees. Additionally, HR teams are integral to staff retention. Attrition can be costly if trading companies often need to rehire and retrain employees. Effective HR departments work with internal desks to prevent high employee turnover.

HR can also serve as an external face of the company, although large firms sometimes have dedicated public relations departments for corporate communications.

Ultimately, HR helps ensure that trading firms attract, develop, and retain the talent that underpins their success in a highly competitive industry.

Environmental, Social, and Governance

With the global shift toward renewable energy and a focus on environmental stewardship, ESG teams play a central role in trading houses. Trading houses face pressure to protect their public image and also to secure financing, with banks increasingly expecting meaningful ESG commitments to extend credit.

In recent years, larger traders have begun publishing annual reports detailing their ESG approach, covering carbon controls and scope-3 disclosures, safety protocols, due diligence requirements, and greenhouse gas tracking. These metrics are vital to building public trust and the continued financial stability of trading companies.

As the global economy transitions, ESG teams will grow in influence, shaping how trading companies access capital, manage risk, and sustain their licenses to operate.

Chapter Summary

- Commodity trading firms are complex organizations composed of many departments, each playing a vital role in the success of the business.
- Although it is the front-office teams that are often most visible, they rely heavily on the support and expertise that other departments provide to ensure trades are executed correctly.
- From finance and operations to risk and legal, along with many other departments, all contributing and working together toward achieving the long-term goals of the company.
- Understanding the function and interactions between each of these roles is essential in understanding how a trading firm operates and how your role fits into the larger picture.

Guns Drawn at Dusk

Working late is relatively commonplace in the commodities industry. Whether it's making sure P&Ls are reported accurately at month-end, dealing with another unexpected problem that comes up when you were thinking about leaving for the day, or simply being overloaded and trying to catch up, these challenges are not unusual.

On the risk desk, working late can be a daily occurrence. A crucial role on the hedge desk is ensuring that the company's outright exposure remains within limits. This task is so critical in preventing losses that staff cannot head home for the night until books are square. This often involves hours of investigative work piecing together information from different sources until you have an answer.

One such evening, a colleague and I had been staring at our screens for longer than any eye-doctor recommends when we realized just how dark and empty the office had become. Still, we had a job to finish and it did not matter how loudly our stomachs grumbled with hunger or how late it was.

After finally finding the contract that was causing an error in our hedge card and sending an email to the operator that had forgotten to update the system, which may have included language deemed "inappropriate" in 2025, we grabbed our coats and headed for a well-earned nightcap.

As we stepped into the elevator, casually chatting about how England would definitely win the upcoming 2010 World Cup, we were not prepared for what would meet us at the ground floor. As the elevators opened we were greeted by a whole team from the local Swiss police unit. Full tactical gear, guns drawn, instructions being yelled to get down on the floor.

"Jetzt! Schnell!"

I should have paid more attention in my eighth grade German class.

It turns out that the office manager had not realized Nick and I were still in the office and had set the alarm when leaving the building. When we finally stood up from our desks we triggered the motion detectors and silent alarm. If there's one thing the Swiss are known for it is their efficiency, and the speed of the response of their armed police unit is a testament to that.

After explaining that we were employees and were not trying to steal trade secrets, we were let go. As we sat at the bar afterward, hands still a bit shaky, we agreed that we should probably tell the office manager if we were working that late again.

In commodities, you quickly learn that a small oversight can create outsized consequences. Whether that's an unsquare hedge card leading to a loss, or accidentally triggering a SWAT response team on your way out of the building.

4. Know Your Counterparty

Commodity trading is full of jargon, but know your counterparty (KYC) is one of the most important concepts in the industry. It is not simply an acronym but a core process that underpins every transaction.

When a commodity company agrees to do business with another, it is incumbent upon them to perform specific checks to understand exactly who it is doing business with. The term for these checks is KYC.

Failure to establish proper KYC procedures can lead companies to engage with businesses involved in criminality, that are sanctioned, and that involve high risk, creating huge exposure - financially, legally, and reputationally. It is therefore critical that all employees strictly follow KYC procedures.

A bedrock of the KYC procedure is a company background check, similar to the due diligence a bank conducts when you apply for a credit card. The bank would not simply agree to lend you money without performing some due diligence.

Each company has their own unique way of doing this, but they all boil down to gaining the same goal: gaining information. In the global environment of commodity trading, these checks need to go beyond domestic borders because many companies or individuals are barred from trading internationally.

As part of this background check, the company ownership will be assessed. Who are the principal shareholders of the company? Most commodity companies are privately held which means their ownership details may not be publicly known. Trading companies need to establish who the ultimate beneficial owners of any transaction would be, before entering into contracts.

Sometimes ownership structure involves multiple companies. This is not inherently risky, but the whole ownership chain must be established to ensure compliance with the law.

Private companies are usually private for a reason - they do not like their information available in the public sphere. Nondisclosure agreements are standard in the industry to allow companies to share information without broader disclosure.

Typical checks on private companies will be more stringent KYC procedures for public companies. For a company to be listed on a major stock exchange, that exchange will have already conducted extensive due diligence. Major shareholders will be publicly known and well-audited financial results are accessible to the public.

Public companies are under more stringent scrutiny than private companies further reducing risk. This does not mean that dealing with public companies is entirely without risk, but it does mean from a criminal perspective that it is safe to proceed with business.

Once ultimate ownership of a group has been established, the other aspects of the company must be assessed.

Assessment would include determining how many years has the company been in existence. A relatively new company may not have much of a reputation, good or bad. Either way, a new company can be harder to assess than a well-established one that has been in the industry for decades and has an industry-wide reputation.

Determining the size of the corporation is also essential. Is this a five-person operation or a 5,000 employee business? The size of the company can help determine the level of risk in doing business. It is much harder for large companies to fly under the radar of regulators and other scrutiny. However, it is much easier for smaller organizations to be involved in practices that pose a risk to doing business with them.

It is also equally critical to know the nature of all of the company's businesses. Companies are often multi-faceted - just because it is transacting in a commodity or region you wish to trade in, does not mean this is its only business stream. When assessing a company, even if the scope of your specific proposal is narrow, the company must be analyzed as a whole to ensure compliance.

The scope of the business must also be determined - is this going to be a one-off deal or a long-term relationship? One-off deals, while not inherently risky, carry a higher level of risk than long-term business. There is minimal recourse if a new company reneges on a single spot deal. But having the prospect of a long-term agreement can add some comfort when opening a new account.

The volume of the deal must be known. Some companies have minimum volume requirements to transact with a counterparty. Not only are unit costs lower when transacting at higher volumes, but if a large volume of business is being discussed there is usually less chance of nonperformance than on a lower volume deal. While fraud can of course happen on a large scale, high-volume business tends to be performed with large, well-established companies, reducing counterparty risk.

The owners of a company are not the only key figures who need to be established. The key officers and management will also be assessed to ensure they are not subject to any restrictions or have negative reputations that could create transactional risk.

It must also be determined if the new counterparty has any anti-bribery and anti-corruption policies in place. Companies are increasingly required to have established policies that reduce the risk of illegality to demonstrate their reputation.

There will also be a financial health check performed on any new counterparty. Financial statements provide insights into both past and future financial performance. Particularly if a deal involves offering extended payment terms, financial assessments are vital. Even private companies can be assigned a credit score based on their financials which will influence the ability to offer credit terms. The result of this financial analysis will often influence the accepted level of trade volume and whether business can proceed with the counterparty.

Banking details are a pivotal part of KYC checks. For a company to maintain an account with a major bank, the bank itself will have performed strong due diligence. This doesn't mean KYC procedures do not need to be followed, but it does provide an additional layer of security that a reputable bank has already made primary checks.

In contrast, if a company banks with a relatively unknown organization, it can raise questions and trigger additional scrutiny. Some banks that are on sanction lists would prevent business being conducted, even if the counterparty itself were not sanctioned. Banking details will also determine the currency a counterparty must pay, or be paid in, which can add complexity and risk to transactions.

For as global as it is, the commodities industry is relatively tight-knit. This means that most companies in each space have reputations - for better or worse. Companies will pay keen attention to market reputation. Even if a new company is not personally known to the group, a reputation for fraud or illegality in the market will prompt additional checks or halt new business altogether.

There is no standard KYC procedure across the industry. Even if you have followed strict KYC policies at a previous company, you must still familiarize yourself with the procedures at your current company because there can be differences - some subtle and some large - within the industry.

Even with the strictest KYC procedures, a company is only protected in the long run when its employees stay vigilant and are empowered to raise red flags when they see potential issues. Companies that have no prior history of misconduct can still fall victim to rogue traders. Several high-profile cases in recent years resulted in losses of hundreds of millions of dollars because KYC procedures were not followed. Conversely, stringent KYC procedures have saved companies from equally large losses by flagging dangerous counterparties before deals were executed.

Employees must understand that the KYC is only the first step in protecting the company from negative consequences. The industry will always face fraudulent actors looking to make quick profits at others' expense. Employees should remain alert for something that looks or feels unusual and should never be afraid to raise an issue or seek further clarification.

Chapter Summary

- KYC procedures are an essential part of commodity trading
- Trading companies use them to mitigate legal, financial, and reputational risks when opening new counterparties.
- Effective KYC procedures involve examining the ownership structure, financial health, legal standing, banking relationships, and market reputation of potential counterparties.
- The size, frequency, and nature of the proposed business are also considered when assessing counterparty risk.
- KYC procedures do not stop at onboarding. Employees must be empowered to raise red flags when they encounter potential issues to prevent adverse outcomes before they occur.

One-Hundred-Year Egg

Most of you will have experienced eating Chinese food or at least the Western version of it. Fried rice, noodles, crispy duck pancakes, you know the drill. So when Anthony was presented with the one-hundred-year egg, to say he was taken aback would be an understatement.

Having always wanted to visit China, an upcoming team meeting provided the perfect opportunity to have someone else cover the airfare. Still, this wouldn't be all fun and games. In addition to performing his regular trading duties from a time zone six hours ahead, he would also have to put in face time with various clients.

At one such client dinner, conversation flowed as did the *baijiu*. For those unfamiliar, baijiu is the number-one selling alcohol in the world but relatively unheard of outside of China. It is incredibly potent, typically around 55% alcohol. This dinner was getting interesting.

After a brief conversation in Mandarin that he was not privy to, Anthony noticed grins shooting his way from around the table. *Excellent,* his baijiu-enhanced mind thought. *I'm impressing them already*.

Five minutes later, a hush fell over the crowd as a single dish was brought into the room and placed before the guest of honor. The one-hundred-year egg, or century egg, is a preserved egg cured in clay, ash, salt, quicklime, and rice hulls for weeks to months. This process turns the egg jet black on the outside, grey on the inside, with a pungent smell of ammonia and sulfur. It is a delicacy in China.

Anthony knew that respecting culture was extremely important, and surely this couldn't be any worse than some of the food he'd put away during his university days.

It was much, much worse.

Still, armed with baiju-induced courage he continued eating to the delight of the locals who watched with a mix of joy and admiration.

In China there is an etiquette of *not* finishing your plate to show your host has given you enough food. Let's just say this wouldn't be an issue with this particular dish.

Understanding cultures is a huge part of commodity trading. Whether that's knowing how to take and present a business card with two hands, attempting a few phrases in the local language, or forcing yourself to eat something you have absolutely no interest in eating.

Paying attention to cultural differences can make a huge difference in relationships. And small gestures often go a long way to building trust and business.

5. Logistics

As discussed in chapter 2, logistics expertise plays a major role in the existence of commodity traders. Regardless of your role in the industry, a solid understanding of logistics is vital to your long-term success. Whether you are in financial or physical trading, in front, middle, or back-office, logistics affects all aspects of commodities from prices to deliveries.

Commodity companies are responsible for transporting thousands of tons of material across the globe, using multiple methods. Each of these modes of transport will have specific nuances - many of which are covered in this chapter.

Different costs, benefits, and risks associated with each form of transport must be understood to avoid unexpected and costly delays when moving products from one location to the next. And although there are simple trades that do not involve physically transporting material, most commodity trades involve at least one form of transport, often several.

Employees at trading companies spend time developing relationships with logistics providers across all modes of transport. Staying on top of market changes and trends allows them to keep costs as low as possible. As we saw throughout the COVID-19 pandemic, logistics costs can be highly inelastic, with bottlenecks occurring regularly and drastically affecting freight rates. Without keeping a keen eye on these movements, companies cannot react quickly when changes happen.

Logistics typically account for the largest share of costs under a physical contract, so errors in planning, booking, and executing freight movements can mean the difference between profit and loss.

Vessel Shipments

Vessel shipments account for 70 to 80 percent of all international trade. This makes sense considering the need to cross oceans to reach final consumption points.

Of those shipments, between 20 and 25 percent by volume is shipped on containerized vessels. Bulk cargoes are split between dry bulk such as iron ore, coal, and metal concentrates, which account for 40 to 45 percent by volume; and liquid bulk such as crude oil, liquefied natural gas (LNG), and chemicals, which make up 30 to 35 percent by volume. There is a tiny share of vessel cargo, between 1 and 2 percent shipped by break bulk such as oversized cargo like large machinery. Break bulk can also be used in specific shipments of other commodities like refined metals.

Container Vessels

Container vessels are favored for their efficiency, speed, and versatility. Companies can ship thousands of tons of commodities on hundreds of containers or much smaller volumes in one or two containers. Container shipments offer much flexibility in terms of volume and routes than bulk cargoes do. There are container shipping lanes covering most ports globally. Unlike ports for bulk vessels which need to be of a certain depth to ensure safe docking, most container ports do not face similar constraints.

There are two standard container sizes: twenty-foot and forty-foot, known as twenty-foot equivalent units (TEUs) and forty-foot equivalent units (FEUs). Even though FEUs make up between 60 and 65 percent of global container volume, TEUs are the standard for shipping metal because weight limits are reached well before the container is full.

For commodities requiring a constant, controlled temperature, temperature-controlled containers (reefers) are utilized.

The process for shipping material via containers is relatively straight-forward, but if some simple steps are not followed correctly it can lead to costly delays.

When a product needs to be shipped via vessel, the shipping party will contact a freight forwarder or a shipping line directly. A freight forwarder is essentially a broker that acts as an intermediary between shipping lines and the shipper.

A booking request will be submitted detailing the relevant cargo information, volume, destination, and requested shipment dates. The forwarder or shipping line will check vessel schedules, space availability, and pricing for the shipment, and provide these details to the shipper.

The specific vessel details are an important factor when arranging shipments. Many commodity companies will be bound by conditions in their marine insurance policies, which must be checked before a vessel booking. The age of the vessel, the flag (or country) under which it operates, and any history of accidents - these can all affect whether a company can accept a vessel. For example, it is common for a trader's insurance policy to require all vessels to be under 20 years old to provide coverage.

Outside of the ocean freight rate there are two additional pricing components that must be understood: the currency adjustment factor (CAF) and the bunker adjustment factor (BAF).

Shipping lines are often required to pay costs in local currencies such as port fees and labor, but they usually quote prices in USD. Volatile foreign exchange (FX) rates can erode their margin, so CAF shifts that risk onto the customer. Shipping lines will publish CAF levels either monthly or quarterly depending on FX volatility. It is calculated using a basket of reference currencies utilizing preset formulas or index-linked calculations. It is expressed either as a percentage of the base freight or a flat amount per container or ton.

For example if the base freight per container is $2,000 and CAF is 7 percent, the CAF charge is $140, bringing the total amount per container to $2,140. The final CAF charge is often only known at the time of shipment, not at the time of booking, so swings in the CAF percentage can affect traders' margins. Some carriers will offer fixed-CAF contracts but typically at higher base freight rates.

BAF is a surcharge to cover the cost of bunker fuel, which is one of the most significant operating expenses for shipping lines. Fuel costs can be highly volatile, reacting to global oil prices, geopolitical shocks, and

International Maritime Organization (IMO) regulations. Carriers will separate fuel price risk from the base freight cost.

BAF is usually tied to published bunker fuel indices along with regional fuel price benchmarks. The vessel type, route, and fuel consumption assumptions will also affect BAD, which is revised monthly or quarterly. Similarly to CAF it can be charged as a flat rate per container, per ton, or as a percentage of the base freight cost.

BAF is highly volatile, particularly after IMO 2020 which limited the sulfur content in marine fuel to 0.5 percent from the previous 3.5 percent. A sudden spike in a published fuel index can unexpectedly add from $100 to more than $400 per container unexpectedly.

If the shipper agrees to the shipment terms, they will proceed with booking and will receive a booking confirmation. This confirmation will include details such as the booking reference number; vessel name and voyage number; port of loading and destination; and importantly, the cut-off times for delivery of the containers to the loading dock. Failure to deliver the container on time will incur charges for the shipper. The booking confirmation will also include pickup instructions for the empty containers to be loaded with the shipper's commodity.

When the material is ready to be loaded, the container(s) will be picked up from the container depot. Containers must be inspected at this stage to ensure they are free of damage. If any damage is found, the driver will request a different container. The container is then taken to a warehouse or place of loading where the goods will be "stuffed" - shipping terminology for loaded. Cargo must be secured in the container using dunnage or sometimes lashing or breaching to prevent unexpected movement during the voyage.

Once fully loaded, the container is sealed. This does not simply mean locking the doors. There is a physical seal, like a tag, applied to the container. This seal has a specific recorded number. It is crucial for security and documentation that the seal remains intact until the container reaches its destination. These seals are not designed to prevent being opened but rather to break when opened so they cannot be resealed without the break being clearly visible. If containers arrive at the destination with missing or broken seals, it suggests that the cargo has been tampered with after being loaded at the port.

The stuffed and sealed containers are transported to the port terminal. At the port, the driver will provide the booking details which port staff will check against the paperwork such as shipping instructions, and verified gross mass document. This is a statement from the shipper confirming the total weight of a stuffed container including the cargo, any packaging, and the tare weight of the container. The containers may also be weighed again before being registered into the port's terminal operating system.

The containers are stacked in the port's container yard until the designated vessel arrives.

Containers will be loaded in a specific order based on the goods they contain to ensure ship stability during the voyage - known as the stowage plan, and this is why obtaining exact container weights is critical. The containers are locked into place onboard - both to one another and to the ship's structure.

Terminal handling charges will be paid to load containers onto a vessel, and again to discharge them from a ship at the destination. The Incoterms of the physical contract will dictate whether the shipper or the buyer (if one exists) pays these charges. It is essential they are not overlooked because they will typically be supplemental to the ocean freight rate and must be included in any profit and loss calculations.

Once loading is completed the ship's officers will verify the load list. After any customs and immigration approvals have been granted the vessel will be cleared to depart and a bill of lading (BOL or B/L) will be issued. A BOL is a legally recognized title document that lists the contents and weights of each container, and the owner of the goods. Only the named owner (or another party the owner endorses) will be able to pick up the material at the port of discharge.

Dry-Bulk Vessels

The process for booking and loading bulk cargo differs from container-vessels. Freight contracts for bulk vessels are negotiated with the charterer or shipping agent. A charterer is a company that has hired the vessel from the owners for a specific period or a specific voyage.

The key terms such as cargo material, quantity, port of loading and discharge, freight rates, and laycan dates are agreed. The laycan date is extremely important because it defines the window in which the vessel must arrive at the port of loading.

There are serious consequences for the charterer if the vessel does not arrive during the agreed laycan window and the shipper may be within their rights to cancel the booking. Likewise, there are substantial penalties for the shipper if loading delays cause the vessel to remain at the port of loading past the last date of the laycan.

Based on the material volume, the vessel type and specifications are also confirmed. Bulk vessels have specific designations based on their max capacities. Below are the most common ship sizes and their capacities. Bulk vessel capacities are listed in deadweight tonnage (DWT), which is the maximum weight including everything the ship transports - cargo, fuel, provisions and stores, and the crew and passengers:

- Handysize: 10,000-40,000 DWT: Handysize vessels are more flexible and can access smaller ports with tighter draft restrictions
- Handymax: 40,000-50,000 DWT: Slightly larger than Handysize but still designed for smaller port access.
- Supramax: 50,000-60,000 DWT: Handymax and supramax vessels are equipped with onboard cranes and can call at ports with less infrastructure.
- Panamax: 60,000-80,000 DWT: Panamax vessels were designed to fit through the old Panama Canal locks.
- Kamsarmax: 80,000-85,000 DWT: Named after the Port of Kamsar in Guinea, kamsarmax were designed to be the largest vessel to dock in the port.

- New Panamax: 85,000-120,000 DWT: These vessels were adjusted to fit the new Panama Canal locks after the 2016 expansion.
- Capesize: 120,000-200,000 DWT: These vessels are too large for the Panama or Suez Canals and must go around the Cape of Good Hope in South Africa, or Cape Horn in Chile.
- Very Large Ore Carrier (VLOC): 200,000-320,000 DWT and Ultra Large Ore Carrier (ULOC): 320,000-400,000+ DWT: VLOC and ULOC vessels are primarily used to transport iron ore from Brazil or Australia to Asia. They are limited to deepwater ports with specialized infrastructure.

If the terms of the physical contract require it, the vessel will be nominated by the shipper to the buyer of the goods for approval. The shipper or buyer may face similar constraints regarding the age and flag of the proposed vessel as container shipments, dictated by their insurance policies. Once any approvals are given, a fixture notice is issued to formalize the booking.

The bulk cargo is prepared for loading at the storage facility while awaiting the vessel. Once the vessel arrives, it will be prepared for loading, which may involve clearing and inspecting the holds. Some companies may require a preloading survey of the vessel to certify readiness.

Bulk vessels will dock at a bulk handling berth - this must be deep enough to accommodate the vessel and equipped with the necessary infrastructure such as conveyor belts or loaders that can load the vessel accordingly.

The cargo is distributed evenly inside the holds to maintain the ship's balance during the voyage. This is extremely important given the length of some voyages, and the varying sea conditions they have to navigate. It would be extremely dangerous for the crew should a ship become unbalanced during a voyage.

The draft of a ship is the vertical distance between the waterline and the lowest point of the hull; it essentially informs how deep the ship sits in the water. Draft surveys are taken before and after loading to measure the exact cargo weight by calculating the vessel's displacement - the weight of the water it displaces.

Once material has been loaded, hatches are sealed to prevent any contamination or loss on the voyage. Documentation such as the BOL and cargo manifest is issued, along with any inspection or survey reports. The vessel will then depart provided customs and port authorities have cleared the ship for sailing.

Breakbulk Vessels

Breakbulk shipping looks more like dry-bulk shipping than container shipping but there are crossovers between the two. Breakbulk is sometimes used to ship refined metal in large volumes, where it is more efficient and cost-effective to charter an entire hold or breakbulk vessel than use hundreds of containers. Breakbulk vessels have different holds within the same vessel, each designed to accommodate specific types of cargo.

The shipper will arrange for shipment via a shipping line or freight forwarder. The vessel booking will depend on the cargo type, volume, dimensions, port of loading and discharge, and any delivery deadlines.

Once the freight rate is agreed and the booking is confirmed, a booking confirmation is issued. The cargo is organized at the shipper's warehouse or storage yard before the vessel's arrival.

Once the vessel is docked, the cargo is lifted by cranes or forklifts and placed onto the vessel. The cargo is secured inside the hold using ropes, chains, and dunnage to prevent movement during the voyage. Terminal staff ensure that the cargo loading plan is followed to account for balance, stability, and weight distribution.

Once the cargo has been securely loaded and stowed, a mate's receipt signed by the chief officer confirms that the cargo was loaded in the agreed condition, and BOLs are issued. After any customs documentation is completed and clearance is granted, the vessel will be cleared for departure.

Wet-Bulk Vessels

Wet-bulk vessels are also known as tankers. As the name suggests, these vessels are designed to carry liquid commodities such as crude oil, refined petroleum products, liquified natural gas (LNG), chemicals, and edible oils.

There are many similarities in the booking process between dry and wet bulk vessels. The key terms such as cargo material, quantity, port of loading and discharge, freight rates, and laycan dates are agreed between the shipper and the charterer.

But there are differences in the classes of vessel between dry bulk and tanker:

- Handysize: 10,000-40,000 DWT: Used for small ports or short-haul voyages.
- Medium Range (MR): 40,000-55,000 DWT.
- Long Range 1 (LR1): 55,000-80,000 DWT
- Long Range 2 (LR2): 80,000-160,000 DWT. LR1 and LR2 vessels are used for longer, or intercontinental voyages.
- Aframax: 80,000-120,000 DWT.
- Suezmax: 120,000-200,000 DWT: These are the largest tankers that can pass through the Suez Canal fully loaded.
- Very Large Crude Carrier (VLCC): 200,000-320,000 DWT: Widely used in the trade of crude oil, particularly from the Middle East to Asia and Europe.
- Ultra Large Crude Carrier (ULCC): 320,000-550,000 DWT: These are rarer than VLCC vessels as they are limited to a handful of ports globally. VLCC vessels can carry over half a million tons of crude oil.

Given the environmental impacts of liquid cargoes, tanker bookings often require additional vetting. Major terminals maintain approved vessel lists that traders can reference. Liquid chartering contracts require more stringent safety clauses, and cargo-specific material safety data sheets (MSDS) are often required.

Handling liquid cargo requires different considerations than dry cargo. Liquid cargoes are pumped from main supply pipelines either directly into shore pipelines and then onto vessels, or first into onshore storage tanks before being loaded onto vessels.

Some US Gulf Coast refineries load refined products straight from refinery pipelines onto product tankers. Crude oil export terminals are also connected directly to long-distance pipelines in Russia, the US, and West Africa that can bypass intermediate storage. However, while liquid cargoes *can* be pumped directly from main supply pipelines into short pipelines and then onto vessels, several challenges accompany this method.

The scheduling of pipeline supply, vessel arrival, and pumping rates must align perfectly. If any point in the chain faces delays, the pipeline flow must be curtailed or rerouted.

In most cases, liquid cargo is first pumped into onshore storage tanks before loading onto a vessel. While costs can increase because of extra handling, the storage acts as a buffer to smooth out any timing mismatches between pipeline deliveries and tanker schedules.

Onshore storage also allows for blending of cargoes such as crude oil grades and refined products. It also allows quality and safety checks to be performed before cargo is exported.

Some large export hubs allow both methods, with most volume flowing from storage tanks, but supplemental volumes can be pumped directly from pipelines if timing allows.

Determining the volumes loaded onto a liquid vessel also differs from dry bulk. Where dry bulk uses draft surveys, tankers use ullage reports or shore flow meters.

Ullage is the empty space between the top of a liquid cargo and the reference point at the top of the tank - the ullage point. Instead of measuring the volume of cargo in the tank, you measure the space left above it.

A measuring tape, often weighted and sometimes electronic, is lowered through a designated hatch. The measured ullage is compared to tank calibration tables and the reading is converted into a cargo volume.

Shore flow meters are devices installed in port loading or discharge pipelines that measure the volume of liquid cargo passing through them. The advantage of flow meters is that cargo volumes are monitored in real time. They are less manual than ullage and increasingly common in modern ports. However, meters must be calibrated appropriately otherwise results can be disputed.

It is not uncommon for a discrepancy to arise between the ship's figures (ullage) and shore figures (flow meter). The charterparties and physical deal contracts will typically specify which set of figures will govern, for example, "shore figures final."

Once loading is complete, BOLs are issued. Standard customs documents are required for clearance, but additional paperwork is often needed for hazardous cargoes such as crude oil and chemicals. Certificates of origin or sanctions clearances may also be required depending on the destination.

Another unique aspect of shipping liquid cargoes is ship-to-ship transfers, (STS). Large vessels such as VLCCs often cannot berth at specific ports, but they will still be used for cost-efficiency. On these occasions, cargo will be transferred to smaller ships offshore, before final delivery to port. It can also be used to reduce waiting times at congested ports or to blend different cargo grades during STS operations.

During an STS operation the vessels will moor side-by-side and cargo hoses are connected between the manifolds. Pumps transfer cargo while maintaining strict monitoring of flow, pressure, and safety systems. There is a higher risk of oil spills, hose ruptures, or fire when compared to discharging at a terminal, so there is strict regulatory oversight on STS transfers. They are often limited to designated offshore STS zones.

Detention and Demurrage

Detention and demurrage are essential concepts in shipping. Both are forms of penalty charges that arise when agreed time limits are exceeded in shipping contracts.

Demurrage applies to bulk and container shipments. On bulk vessels, demurrage can apply at the port of loading and discharge. Demurrage will be incurred if cargo loading is delayed, or takes longer than planned, keeping the vessel in the port beyond the agreed laytime - the agreed number of days allowed for loading or discharge. This is the same at the port of discharge if the vessel cannot depart its destination within the agreed laytime.

Efficient and well-organized loading and unloading of vessels is imperative to avoid demurrage costs. The charterer will pay demurrage to the shipowner, and this cost will be passed on to the shipper. It is a rent cost for keeping the vessel waiting. The specific demurrage rate will be predetermined at the time of booking the vessel.

In container shipping, demurrage applies while containers are inside the port, and detention applies while containers are outside the port of discharge.

If upon arrival at the port of discharge, containers sit too long inside the port before being picked up or delivered, demurrage is applicable. The number of free days is negotiated as part of the initial freight booking. Demurrage will be applied if the containers remain at discharge port beyond these free days. For example, if five free days have been granted at the port and containers remain for eight days before being picked up, three days of demurrage will be charged to the shipper by the shipping line. Demurrage costs can add up quickly and are part of the reason accurate and efficient BOL document control is crucial.

If containers remain outside the port beyond the free time allowed for unpacking and returning the empty container to the container yard, detention is applicable. If containers are not returned on time, the shipping line cannot charge a different shipper for its use on a different voyage. Like demurrage, the number of detention-free days is negotiated at the point of booking the vessel.

Demurrage and detention costs must be paid immediately if incurred. Because charges accrue daily, payment delays can snowball into high, unexpected costs. In the case of demurrage, these costs need to be paid before the shipping line releases the goods.

Dispatch

Laytime dictates the latest date by which a vessel may load or discharge without incurring additional costs. However, if vessel loading finishes early, allowing for departure before the end of a laycan, the owner may owe the charterer a payment known as dispatch.

Dispatch is effectively a rebate paid by the vessel owner to the charterer for using less laytime than agreed. It encourages efficient terminal operations and incentivizes charterers to complete loading or discharge early. The less time a vessel spends in a port, the more voyages it can make. Where demurrage is a penalty, dispatch is a reward, though usually paid at a lower rate than demurrage is charged, often 50 percent.

For example, if the allowed laytime is five days, but the actual loading takes three days, the unused laytime is two days. Using a demurrage rate of $20,000 per day and a dispatch rate of 50 percent, the dispatch earned would be as follows:

2 * $10,000 = $20,000

For a trader, dispatch can materially improve voyage economics, lowering net freight costs and improving margins.

But not all vessels offer dispatch. Most tanker contracts prioritize safety over speed; dispatch is not the top concern. Maximum pumping rates are set to avoid static electricity buildup; there are mandatory line checks and strict sampling requirements. Tanker owners argue that quick turnaround should *not* be financially incentivized. In tight freight markets some bulk vessel owners refuse to offer dispatch or the rates may be heavily reduced. However, when possible dispatch is always worth negotiating as over the course of a trading year, dispatch earnings can create significant profits.

Trucking

After vessel shipments, truck shipments are the most common method to transport commodities. Trucks play a pivotal role in local and domestic deliveries. They are critical for first-mile and last-mile delivery and are used to move product directly from warehouses to consumers, and from production sites to ports or rail-heads.

While trucks more frequently carry full truckloads, they can also make smaller, customized deliveries known as LTL loads, which stands for less-than-truckloads.

Trucks can carry a wide range of commodities, from metal to agricultural products. Tanker trucks are required to carry liquid commodities to final destinations.

For nonliquid commodities, there are two main types of trucks: flatbeds and tractor-trailers. Flatbeds have a flat, open bed with no sides or roof. They are ideal for carrying loads that are too wide for enclosed trailers, and they are also used to transport containers to port as they can be loaded from multiple angles. Flatbeds are used to transport steel, lumber, and machinery. Cargo is frequently exposed during transit so if weather is a concern, flatbeds can be tarped to keep material dry.

Tractor-trailers have a cab and a separate trailer that is hooked onto the cab. They have fixed dimensions and can only be loaded from the rear. Unlike flatbeds, trailers are covered so weather is not a concern. Some tractor-trailers specialize in transporting cargo at set temperatures to ensure products do not spoil before reaching their destination. These are known as refrigerated trucks, or reefers.

Tanker trucks have a sealed cylindrical tank mounted on the trailer. They often have multiple compartments that allow for several grades of product to be carried at once. They are fitted with hoses and pumps for direct loading or unloading from, or into storage tanks, pipelines, or facilities. Depending on the cargo, tanks may be insulated, pressurized, or temperature-controlled.

Wherever you are moving material on a truck, be it from a port to a warehouse, from a warehouse to a port, from a production site, or to a final consumer, the first stage is booking the transport. This can be done directly with a trucking company, through a truck broker, or with a storage company that provides trucking services. Brokers do not typically own trucks; instead they utilize a network of truck owners and companies to fulfill shipments. Storage facilities may also lack their own fleets and may use local contacts for trucking services.

Booking details will involve negotiating a rate for the delivery, pickup locations and dates, cargo type, volume, and any special handling requirements. The weight of the goods being transported is critical. While companies will usually want to load trucks to maximum capacity, the maximum weights allowed per truck can vary by country or even region to region.

For example, on US highways, the gross vehicle weight (GVW) allowed for a double-axle truck is 80,000 lbs. Given that most trucks weigh around 34,000–36,000 lbs when empty, the maximum load they can carry is about 45,000 lbs, or around 20 mt. However, in Europe, the standard GVW is 40 mt, allowing a maximum cargo weight closer to 25 mt. Understanding these key differences is crucial, particularly if you are involved in shipping to multiple geographical locations.

Once the trucking has been arranged, release instructions will need to be sent to the storage location (if shipping from storage), so they can prepare the material for pickup and confirm that delivery slots are available. Storage facilities will not allow loading without explicit instructions from the cargo owner. Releases will need to include the trucking company and material-specific details that can be cross-checked upon loading. Facilities will also confirm that there are no bank holds over the material that would need to be before prior to arranging loading.

These steps are similar to arranging transport from a producer - the producer will still need to be informed of which trucking company has been engaged to fulfill the logistics.

Once a truck has been booked, it will arrive at the loading destination on the pre-agreed date. Material will be loaded onto the truck by the storage facility or loading location - truckers do not actively load the trucks themselves. They will however be responsible for ensuring cargo is properly secured and stabilized for road safety.

Once loaded, the driver will sign a delivery note that describes the contents of the load. This is also known as a truck BOL. While this will list the contents of the load, unlike a vessel BOL, it is not used as an industry standard title document. We will cover title documents in detail in Chapter Nine.

Trucks are usually weighed both light and heavy to determine the load's specific weight. Weighing trucks can provide companies with confirmation that the material weighs what the documentation states. These weights can also be used to verify the accuracy of the truck BOL.

If trucks are being used to carry materials across international borders, such as deliveries in continental Europe, shippers must ensure that all customs documentation is complete and accurate. Delays at borders can lead to higher trucking fees and delays in delivery to consumers, so paperwork should be organized and transmitted well in advance of any border crossings.

Once trucks reach their destination, receipt is confirmed with a signed proof of delivery (POD). The recipient confirms that the truck has arrived with the goods that are listed on the truck BOL. Importantly, the POD does not prevent the recipient from challenging the delivered goods at a later stage if they believe them to differ in content or quality from what was listed on the BOL. A POD is merely confirmation that the truck arrived and was unloaded at the destination.

Rail

Rail shipments can offer a cost-effective way to transport goods over long, inland distances compared with trucking. Rail lines are often used to ship from mine sites to warehouses or ports. A railcar can carry significantly more volume than a truck - typically a railcar will be able to carry 60–90 mt of material per car.

Rail shipments can be booked either directly with a national railway company, through storage providers, or with other freight forwarders. As with other forms of transportation, bookings will confirm the freight rate, commodity, cargo weight, and wagon type.

Different wagons are used depending on the cargo: open or covered cars for bulk materials, tank wagons for liquid commodities, and specialized refrigerated railcars (reefers) for perishable goods. Vessel containers can also be loaded directly onto railcars, just like flatbed trucks, for intermodal transport to or from ports.

Once a booking is made, empty wagons are delivered to a loading terminal. Releases for the material will be sent by the shipper stating the material to be loaded and shipping instructions. Loading for a railcar must follow specific guidelines to prevent overloading or uneven distribution.

Once loaded, a railway bill - the rail equivalent of a BOL - is issued. Like truck BOLs but unlike vessel BOLs, a railway bill is not considered a title document but a statement of carriage. Railcars will pass over weighbridges to verify cargo both at loading and discharge points.

One often overlooked aspect of rail logistics is that not all railways use the same track gauge - the distance between the inner faces of the rails. While it seems like a minor detail, crossing borders with different gauges can introduce delays, additional costs, and operational adjustments. When a shipment reaches a border where the gauge changes, two solutions are common:

- Transloading is most common where cargo is physically transferred from one wagon type to another.
- A bogie exchange where wagons are hydraulically lifted and the wheelsets (bogies) are swapped to match the new gauge.

Both solutions add handling costs that traders must account for.

The borders of Poland, Slovakia, and Hungary with Ukraine and Belarus are major gauge breaks. This affects rail flows of metals, coal, fertilizers, oil products, and agricultural commodities and can create bottlenecks during high-transit periods such as harvest season in the Black Sea.

While rail shipments are slower and less flexible than truck shipments, requiring significantly more infrastructure to make them possible, they can be more cost-effective over longer distances because of the larger payloads and lower fuel consumption per mile. Rail also produces fewer emissions than trucks, which can be advantageous for any ESG reporting a company makes.

<u>Barges</u>

Barges are less common globally than trucks or vessels, but are widely used in regions with ample waterways such as the Rhine River in Europe, the Mississippi River in North America, and rivers in parts of Asia. Barges can be an efficient and cost-effective way of moving large volumes of material at a relatively low cost.

A single barge can carry as little as 1,200 mt and as much as 2,500 mt of material. Pushed barge convoys can move over 10,000 mt, equivalent to hundreds of trucks or more than one hundred railcars.

Barge terminals are frequently located near prominent production facilities, warehouses, and ports. While barge loading and destination options are limited by rivers' pathways, compared to trucks that can navigate essentially anywhere inland, barges can be a highly effective method of transport.

Different barges are utilized depending on the commodity being transported. Dry cargo barges typically carry loose material such as metal concentrates and are equipped with covers to protect cargo from weather. Open hopper barges have a large central hold and are also used for bulk cargoes, though they provide no weather protection and therefore require tarping for sensitive materials.

Liquid commodities can also be transported in specialized tank barges, which have multiple compartments that allow for a single barge to carry different types or grades of material. These compartments also prevent side-to-side sloshing which could compromise the barge's stability.

While not as common as reefer trucks, railcars, or containers, there is increasing demand for temperature-controlled barges, used to transport certain chemicals and agricultural products. However, it is also frequent for temperature-controlled containers to be transported on barges rather than utilizing a temperature-controlled barge.

As with vessel shipments, barging begins with booking space either via a barge operator, a freight forwarder, or often a storage company that will also handle the loading of the material. Freight rates will be negotiated, and origin and destination terminals will be confirmed along with cargo type, volume, draft requirements, and a loading schedule.

The shipper will send material releases accordingly to ensure the correct material is prepared and available for shipment upon the barge's arrival. Barges will be loaded by cranes, conveyor belts, or front loaders for bulk commodities, and pipelines for liquid commodities. Vessel-to-barge transfers may also be utilized for liquid commodities.

Once the barge has been loaded, a loading certificate and a BOL are issued. Barge BOLs do not serve as title documents but are receipts of goods and transport contracts.

One downside to barge shipments is that transit times can be severely affected by weather, making barge transport more vulnerable to seasonal disruptions than rail or trucking. Dry spells can cause riverways to fall below the draft needed to carry barges; riverways can also freeze, trapping barges in transit. Too much rain can also cause barges to experience delays if currents become too strong to navigate safely or cause clearance issues at bridges.

Barge contracts need to be carefully negotiated and monitored to ensure all parties are aware of any additional costs that delays may cause. I once had a barge stuck frozen on the river for seven weeks. The delay caused issues for my consumer and the final costs far exceeded what it would have cost to simply truck the material from the start.

Once the material reaches the destination terminal, it is offloaded by the terminal operator, and unless the terminal is the final consumer destination, it will be further transported for storage or onward delivery.

Pipelines

Pipelines are a critical mode of transportation for liquid commodities such as crude oil, natural gas, and certain chemicals. Unlike trucks, rail, or barges which move commodities in batches, pipelines enable continuous flow, making them one of the most efficient and cost-effective ways to move huge volumes over long distances once the infrastructure is in place. Pipelines are not just a domestic infrastructure, many flow across borders, and in some cases, even between continents.

In regions such as North America, Russia, and the Middle East, pipelines carry more volume of oil and gas than any other form of inland transport. They connect production fields to refineries, storage facilities, and export terminals.

Pipeline capacity (the volume that can be transported) depends on diameter, length, and pumping infrastructure. A large crude oil pipeline can move hundreds of thousands of barrels per day, far exceeding what a fleet of trucks or railcars could carry. For example, the Druzhba pipeline carries more than a million barrels of crude oil per day across multiple European countries.

Natural gas pipelines are measured in terms of cubic feet or cubic meters of flow, with some of the largest lines transporting billions of cubic feet per day.

To use a pipeline, companies book line space - the right to move a certain volume during a scheduled period. Nominations are submitted in advance indicating the volume they intend to ship. If nominations exceed available capacity, pipelines may be prorated, meaning each shipper gets a reduced allocation.

Rates in pipelines are called tariffs and are charged per barrel or per unit for gas. The term tariff refers to a government regulation requiring pipeline companies to act as common carriers. In countries such as the United States, Canada, and EU member states, pipeline owners must offer service to all customers under the same terms. However, other regions have no such regulatory requirements for setting or approving tariffs.

Pipeline operations require coordination to ensure steady and safe flows. For crude and refined product pipelines, different commodities can often be shipped in sequence, known as batching. For example, a pipeline might send gasoline, then jet fuel, then by diesel. Small buffer zones, known as interface volumes, separate the products to minimize contamination.

Line-fill - the volume of product required to keep the pipeline full - is an important consideration. Shippers may need to contribute, or buy into this volume before they can begin moving their own product. This line-fill volume remains locked in the system permanently, effectively tying up working capital that traders must account for.

Pipeline maintenance is carried out using devices called pigs, which are sent through the pipeline to clean or inspect it.

Unlike vessels or trucks, pipelines do not issue bills of lading. Instead, pipeline tickets or receipts are generated to confirm the volume delivered into and out of the system. While not title documents, these receipts, in combination with storage tank or export receipts, serve as evidence of delivery and form the basis of payment documentation.

Pipelines are generally safer and cheaper per mile than other methods, but they come with unique risks. Leaks or ruptures can cause significant environmental damage. Theft by tapping into pipelines is also a recurring issue in some regions.

Pipelines are also fixed infrastructure. So once built, they cannot be easily rerouted. Any political, regulatory, or environmental disruption can bottleneck supply. For example, following the invasion of Ukraine, Russia shut down and limited the flow through multiple pipelines to Europe. The Nord Stream 1 pipeline, which runs under the Baltic Sea to Germany, had its gas flow progressively reduced by Russia until it was completely halted in late August 2022. In September 2022, explosions damaged Nord Stream 1 and Nord Stream 2, rendering them both inoperable. Subsequently, gas prices rose sharply across Europe as countries scrambled to replace Russian supply from other sources such as LNG from the United States and pipeline gas from Norway.

In practice, pipelines rarely operate in isolation. They connect to storage tanks, refineries, and ports, where products are transferred to vessels, barges, trucks, or railcars. For crude oil exports in particular, pipeline-to-terminal connections form the final stage before tankers are loaded for international shipments.

Multimodal

In practice, moving commodities from one point to another requires more than one mode of transport.

A company may use railcars to move a product from a producer to a warehouse, trucks to move that material from the warehouse to the port, and a vessel to transport it to the final destination for consumption. Becoming familiar with all modes of transport, regardless of how frequently you will be required to use them will help separate you in this field.

You must also get comfortable negotiating with storage facilities, forwarders, and transport owners. These costs are not typically negotiated by front-office teams, but by the middle-office teams that organize shipments. Spending time building relationships with these teams, monitoring market movements, and mastering multi-modal logistics are among the best ways to add value as a commodity professional.

Surveying and Supervision

Surveying is a common feature across all modes of transport. Shippers will often want an independent surveyor to oversee loading, unloading, or both, regardless of how the material is being transported. In fact, some physical contracts explicitly require an independent surveyor's report to make payment for goods, such as document presentation under a letter of credit (LC).

Depending on the request, surveyors may weigh, sample, and analyze goods before loading. We will cover these individual aspects in greater detail in Chapter Ten.

In shipping, one of the risks traders must manage is dead freight - a charge payable when a charterer fails to load the full contracted quantity of cargo. Even if the vessel sails partially empty, the freight is owed as if the full contracted volume were shipped.

For example, if a trader commits load 40,000 mt but loads only 37,500 mt - the shortfall is 2,500mt. At a freight rate of $40/mt, the resulting dead freight is 2,500 * $40 = $100,000

Dead freight is almost never intentional; it is usually the result of poor information or a lack of real-time oversight. The simplest solution to this is investing in on-the-ground surveying and supervision. Surveyors can confirm that the cargo available at the load port matches the contractual minimums, verifying what is actually present, not what is expected. They can verify density and ensure the full tonnage physically fits the vessel. Surveyors can also coordinate with the chief officer to ensure the vessel is safely loaded to the maximum possible draft and monitor truck, rail, or conveyor delivery rates to identify any bottlenecks early.

While reputable storage facilities, forwarders, and other shipping companies can provide some level of security for shipments, independent surveyors add another level of protection against fraud. Unfortunately, in commodities fraud is common so companies are often happy to pay the relatively small surveyor fee to avoid the higher cost of unloading a shipment at the port of discharge only to find incorrect grades; excessive moisture; or, in extreme cases, worthless material disguised as valuable cargo.

Chapter Summary

- Logistics play a critical role in the movement of commodities around the globe.
- While some trades occur without any physical movement, the majority require coordination of at least one type of transportation.
- For international transport, the most common method is vessel shipments - either container or dry and liquid bulk cargoes.
- Each method of transport has its own nuanced booking process, loading and discharge requirements, and documentation, specific to each shipment.
- Familiarity with customs and duty procedures is vital to prevent delays at ports.
- Efficiency is crucial in loading and unloading material to avoid incurring demurrage and detention costs.
- Trucking, rail, and barge shipments are utilized for inland deliveries. Each of these methods offers its own advantages and disadvantages in terms of speed, cost, volume, and infrastructure.
- Pipelines are another critical part of global commodity logistics. They provide the most efficient way to move large volumes of oil, gas, and other liquids over long inland distances, both domestically and across borders.
- Unlike other modes of transport, pipelines offer continuous flow, but also tie up working capital through line-fill and carry unique risks such as leaks, theft, or political disruption.
- Shipping by any method requires excellent coordination among storage facilities, freight forwarders, and discharge locations.
- Strong negotiation skills are needed to secure the most competitive freight rates while maintaining reliability and efficiency.
- Traders use surveyors and inspectors to ensure logistics operations are carried out efficiently and effectively.
- A foundational understanding of logistics is essential for anyone working in physical commodity trading. This knowledge is vital across back, middle, and front-office roles to manage risk and protect margins.

300 Pushup Challenge

Commodity trading often gets a reputation for being full of bravado-driven, intense personalities. For the most part, I haven't found that to be true. This story however, is exactly that.

A conversation was making its way around the office regarding an exercise challenge: 300 pushups in 15 minutes. Sounds simple enough - 20 pushups every minute on the minute. But anyone who has actually tried it knows that by about minute six your arms start feeling like jelly. The alternative is to do as many pushups as possible until you collapse, rest briefly, and then try again.

A few of the guys in the office had already tried and decided it was impossible. Because taking risks is part of the job, betting on this challenge seemed like a no-brainer. But I'm also self-aware, and knew I was not the one who was going to complete it. My colleague Tom however, was extremely fit. Well, his upper body at least, let's just say he didn't mind skipping leg day.

"Tom, I'll back you if you lose and if you win, we'll split the money fifty-fifty"

"OK let me finish up some work and we can go to the gym."

"Erm…so we have to do this now, in the car park, there's a crowd waiting."

There's nothing quite like doing pushups on an oily road while a crowd shouts at you - half of them betting on you to fail and half willing you on. Not because they care about you, but simply because they backed you to win.

Fortunately for my wallet, Tom was victorious and completed the challenge with time to spare. The freight desk however walked away having learned a valuable lesson: Before you take a position, make sure you've done your fundamental research. In this case, a quick look at Tom's shoulders should have given them a clue.

6. Incoterms

To those unfamiliar with Incoterms, they may seem insignificant. However, their importance cannot be understated when it comes to physical contracts. This chapter will explain what Incoterms are, and what they define in physical trading. We will explore the key similarities and differences between the terms and go through the definitions of each in turn.

Incoterms, short for International Commercial Terms, are internationally recognized standardized trading terms published by the International Chamber of Commerce (ICC). These standardized terms are used in physical commodity contracts globally. They are periodically updated, the last time in 2020 at the time of writing. Sometimes outdated Incoterms are removed altogether; other updates may include changes to insurance or more subtle changes. You must be sure you are referencing the most up-to-date version.

Incoterms define the responsibilities of buyers and sellers in physical trading. The Incoterm used in the contract specifies which party is responsible for transportation, insurance, and import and export duties. Incoterms also define the transfer of risk at each stage of the shipment.

Incoterms do not however govern the transfer of title over goods. The transfer of title will usually be defined separately in the sales contract. Incoterms also do not define payment terms, or any breach of contract or liability beyond the physical delivery.

The Incoterm used in a contract will affect the commercial terms, given the various costs and responsibilities imposed on the buyer and seller. Incoterms that place greater cost and risk on the buyer will command a lower premium or a larger discount in the market. Incoterms that place a higher cost and risk on the seller will command higher premiums or lower discounts to market levels.

Understanding the definitions of each Incoterm is very important. Knowing each party's responsibilities in a transaction helps prevent miscommunications, shipment delays, and financing errors. They are the key to understanding the structure of a trade and the exact role that your company needs to play.

Incoterms can be split into four categories:

- E-terms: EXW
- F-terms: FCA, FAS, FOB
- C-terms: CFR, CIF, CPT, CIP
- D-terms: DAP, DPU, DDP

Ex Works

An ex works (EXW) sale puts the least responsibility on the seller. The buyer is responsible for all logistics and the associated risks from the seller's premises onward.

This includes the cost of loading the material onto the desired form of transport, insuring the material in transit, and managing any export customs or duties applicable for international movement.

EXW deals are somewhat common in domestic trades, but less common when the material is moving long distances or through international waters. The buyer in EXW deals must have deep knowledge of the local landscape for either domestic consumption or further international movements.

Free Carrier

Free carrier (FCA) is one of the most widely used Incoterms and is flexible with regards to location. The seller delivers to a carrier or mutually agreed-upon location, which could be a port, terminal, warehouse, or truck.

Risk in an FCA contract transfers once the goods are handed to the carrier, not when they leave the seller's site. The buyer is still responsible for the cost of freight from the carrier to the final destination and insuring the goods through transit. The seller is responsible for export customs clearance, including any duties or taxes in the country of origin. But the buyer is responsible for import customs clearance if the material is moved to another country for consumption.

Free Alongside Ship

Free alongside ship (FAS) is mainly used for bulk shipments. In an FAS contract, the seller is required to transport the goods alongside the vessel at the port. From that point on the buyer assumes responsibility and risk for any further movement of goods. This includes loading and shipping the goods and insuring the material during further transit.

Under an FAS contract, any export customs or duties are paid by the seller, while the buyer bears import duties.

Free on Board

Free on board (FOB) is one of the most commonly used Incoterms in the industry. Under an FOB sale, once the material crosses the ship's rail, all risk and costs transfer to the buyer. The seller is responsible for arranging and paying for all logistics up to the point where the material is loaded onto the vessel.

Under FOB contracts, the vessel nomination itself is arranged by the buyer. The seller pays export duties and the buyer pays import duties.

Cost and Freight

In a cost and freight (CFR) contract the seller pays for the transport to the destination port, even though risk transfers to the buyer once the cargo is loaded on the vessel.

The buyer arranges insurance but the seller will be responsible for the freight cost.

Under CFR deals, the seller typically arranges the freight, despite the risk having passed to the buyer. The seller bears export customs and duty costs, but the buyer will be responsible for those same costs upon import to the final destination

Cost, Insurance, and Freight

Cost, insurance, and freight (CIF) is one of the most widely used Incoterms in the industry. CIF contracts take the seller's obligations one step further than CFR contracts by including the responsibility of insuring the goods throughout their transit.

Sellers will arrange and pay for the movement of goods through to disport, but the risk still transfers to the buyer once the material has been loaded onto a vessel. Because of this, the buyer will often purchase supplemental insurance to cover anything beyond what the seller is obligated to provide. Under Incoterms 2020, the minimum standard of insurance coverage is the Institute Cargo Clause (C), which provides basic coverage and does not cover against many transit risks such as theft, rough handling, or contamination.

The seller bears export customs and duty costs, but the buyer is responsible for these costs upon import to the final destination.

Carriage Paid To

Carriage paid to (CPT) is commonly used for inland or multimodal shipments. Under a CPT contract the seller is responsible for arranging and paying the freight to the named place of destination.

The risk in a CPT contract transfers to the buyer at the point where the goods are delivered to the first carrier in the exporting country. In CPT deals the seller is not required to provide insurance. Buyers will arrange their own insurance to cover their risk during transit.

Export customs clearance and duties are handled by the seller, with the buyer paying these same costs upon importing to the final destination.

Carriage and Insurance Paid To

Where CIF contracts are used for sea voyages, carriage and insurance paid to (CIP) is used for inland and multimodal transport.

The seller is responsible for arranging and paying for the freight to the named place of destination. The seller must also insure the goods through to the named place of destination. However, the risk in a CIP deal transfers from the seller to the buyer upon delivery of the goods to the first carrier at the agreed-upon location in the exporting country.

Buyers in CIP deals will often take out supplemental insurance similar to that in CIF deals. However, under the 2020 Incoterms update, the minimum insurance coverage required by sellers in CIP deals was increased to Institute Cargo Clauses (A). This is an “all-risks” cover, which is broader and includes most accidental loss or damage to goods.

Export customs and duty costs are borne by the seller, with the buyer paying these same costs upon import to the final destination.

Delivered at Place

Under delivered at place (DAP) deals, the seller is responsible for all logistics and costs up to the delivery at the named location, but they are not responsible for unloading the material. The place in this Incoterm can be the buyer’s premises, a port, a storage location, or any mutually agreed point of unloading.

The risk on a DAP deal transfers from the seller to the buyer once the goods reach the place of delivery. The buyer is responsible for any import clearance and duty costs as well as any further logistics costs onward from the named place of delivery. DAP is a flexible term, meaning it can be used for any mode of transport.

Delivered at Place Unloaded

Delivered at place unloaded (DPU) is the only Incoterm where the seller is responsible for unloading the goods at the named place of delivery. The risk of loss and damage to the goods remains with the seller until the material is unloaded.

While the seller's responsibilities include export customs, carriage, and unloading, the buyer takes over responsibility once the goods are unloaded - including any import customs clearance and duties. DPU is also a flexible term, meaning it can be used for any mode of transport.

Delivered Duty Paid (DDP)

In a delivered duty paid (DDP) contract the seller is responsible for all export costs, logistics costs through to the place of delivery, and import or duty costs up until the named place of delivery.

The risk remains with the seller until the point of delivery, however the buyer is responsible for unloading the material. The place of delivery in DDP deals is often the buyer's premises and is more commonly used for domestic rather than international deliveries. Cross-border trades would expose sellers to foreign tax regimes and customs formalities that they may not be set up to handle.

Chapter Summary

- Incoterms are one of the bedrocks of commodity trading.
- A foundational understanding is essential to know which party is responsible for carriage, insurance, export and import clearance, and at what point risk transfers.
- Incoterms range from the largest responsibility on the buyer (EXW), through to the largest responsibilities on the seller (DDP), and everything in between.
- They do not define when title passes, or any payment terms - these issues are defined by the sales contract itself.
- Incoterms have a direct impact on the contractual terms for a business. The more responsibility placed on the seller, the more value a seller will demand. The more responsibility placed on the buyer, the less value a seller can command.
- A key change in the 2020 Incoterms was the higher minimum insurance obligation under CIP contracts (all-risks ICC A) compared to CIF contracts (basic, ICC C).
- Having a broad understanding of all Incoterms is essential, even if you currently have exposure to one or two of them.
- On the following page is a handy chart that lists the responsibilities of the seller and buyer for each Incoterm.

Term	Mode of transport	Delivery / Risk transfers at...	Export clearance	Main carriage	Insurance	Import clearance & duties
EXW Ex-Works	Any	Seller's premises, **before loading**	Buyer	Buyer	Buyer	Buyer
FCA Free Carrier	Any	**Handover to first carrier** at named place	**Seller**	Buyer	Buyer	Buyer
FAS Free Alongside Ship	Sea / inland waterway	**Goods placed alongside vessel** at port of loading	**Seller**	Buyer	Buyer	Buyer
FOB Free On Board	Sea / inland waterway	**Goods loaded on board vessel** at port of loading	**Seller**	Buyer	Buyer	Buyer
CFR Cost & Freight	Sea / inland waterway	**On board vessel** at port of loading	**Seller**	**Seller** pays freight	Buyer	Buyer
CIF Cost, Insurance & Freight	Sea / inland waterway	**On board vessel** at port of loading	**Seller**	**Seller** pays freight	**Seller** provides *minimum* insurance (ICC C)	Buyer
CPT Carriage Paid To	Any	**Handover to first carrier** in exporting country	**Seller**	**Seller** pays freight to named destination	Buyer	Buyer
CIP Carriage & Insurance Paid To	Any	**Handover to first carrier** in exporting country	**Seller**	**Seller** pays freight to named destination	**Seller** provides *all-risks* insurance (ICC A)	Buyer
DAP Delivered At Place	Any	**Arrival of goods at named place of destination**, *not unloaded*	**Seller**	**Seller**	Buyer	Buyer
DPU Delivered At Place Unloaded	Any	**Arrival at named place, goods unloaded**	**Seller**	**Seller**	Buyer	Buyer
DDP Delivered Duty Paid	Any	**Arrival of goods at named place of destination**, *not unloaded*	**Seller**	**Seller**	Buyer	**Seller** pays import clearance & duties

Bomb Squad

P had a reputation as a prankster. In between trading substantial volumes of arb, he always found time to test the desk's sense of humor.

On this particular day, he had popped out to buy a birthday card for his wife. While he was in the shop he spotted one of those novelty cards that make sounds when you open them. This one imitated the gurgling noise of someone drinking.

When he returned to the office, he immediately set about dismantling the card and removing the speaker and pressure pad. His brilliant idea was to place the components under the seat in one of the bathroom stalls so that when someone sat down the noise would play. Classic humor we all expect from senior traders in their forties.

What no one expected was that instead of someone being surprised, laughing, finding the device, and throwing it in the bin, a cleaner discovered it. Initially bemused, and then increasingly alarmed he assumed it was some sort of explosive.

At the time, it was not unheard of for traders to be targeted by environmental groups, so the cleaner took no chances and immediately dialed the bomb squad.

Five minutes later a fully armored unit, complete with robots and sniffer dogs barged into the office. It dawned on P that this particular prank may have gotten a bit out of hand. Bomb squads are not known for their sense of humor, as P discovered while calmly explaining that the device was harmless. His offer to fix the card and give it to one of the police officers only made matters worse.

Commodity trading is high-pressure enough without adding bomb scares to the mix. But it is important to remember to have fun still and enjoy what you do. A large part of that will come down to the desk you sit on and the interactions you have with your team.

Burning out is common in the industry so make sure you find time to see the lighter side…though perhaps it's best if your ideas don't involve shutting buildings down.

It's also worth noting that when you realize you have made a mistake or an error in judgment, you should raise your hand and admit to it. The earlier an error is caught and resolved, the lower the chance of it becoming costly.

A common trait among the best traders in the industry is their quickness to spot a mistake and speed in correcting it, even if it results in a loss.

Failing to spot, trying to ignore, or even hiding a mistake is likely to result in larger losses, and quite possibly a short career in the industry.

7. Storage

While it is not uncommon for commodity trades to involve direct movement from producers through to the end consumer, many commodities will require storage - sometimes briefly, sometimes for extended periods - before reaching their final point of consumption.

Storage takes many forms but broadly falls into two categories:

- Dry bulk storage: Warehouses, stockyards, and silos for refined metals, concentrates, ores, and grains.
- Liquid storage: Tank farms and tank storage facilities for oil, chemicals, and other liquid commodities.

These facilities play a vital role in the global commodity system. They are far more than simple storage solutions, and are commonly integrated into multiple parts of the supply chain.

Part of the reason commodity traders exist is their ability to hold material and distribute it to a global network of customers. They frequently source large volumes of commodities, store them, and deliver to the market when conditions are most favorable. To facilitate this type of trading, access to reliable storage is critical.

Storage locations are typically located near major consumption hubs and global ports. For domestic deliveries, traders may need to store material before final consumption, making storage at this stage necessary. By storing commodities closer to the point of consumption, traders reduce their logistics costs.

Material earmarked for export often requires storing or staging while awaiting loading to the appropriate transport. The largest storage facilities are usually in or around ports to facilitate the transfer of goods to vessels. The same is true for imports - they frequently need to be held before being delivered to a consumer. Having ample storage capacity at key import and export locations minimizes handling costs and provides traders the flexibility to respond to changes in market demand.

In addition to location and logistics, storage of commodities is also shaped by customs and duty regulations. Bonded facilities and foreign trade zones (FTZ) allow companies to defer payment of duties and taxes until materials enter the domestic marketplace.

A bonded storage facility is authorized by a country's customs authorities to hold goods in-bond, allowing goods to be stored without paying duties, provided they remain under customs control. The goods can be re-exported, sold, or processed without formally entering the domestic market. For example, all London Metal Exchange (LME) warehouses operate under bonded status, meaning metal can be stored customs-uncleared, duty-unpaid until it is imported into the country for consumption.

A facility located inside an FTZ is similar to a bonded facility, but it is treated as outside of the customs territory of the country in which it resides. Goods can be stored, blended, or processed without being formally imported.

These options are particularly valuable to traders because they allow them to store material, seize domestic opportunities as they arise, or reexport duty-free if that proves more profitable.

A key distinction between storage facilities across the commodity complex is exchange-approved storage and non-exchange storage. For commodities priced on physically settled exchanges, the delivery takes place at an exchange approved facility. Whether that facility is a warehouse for metal or a tank, terminal, or pipeline for liquid commodities, it must be approved by the exchange.

As part of that approval, the exchange will have inspected the facility to ensure it meets strict operational standards. This includes segregation of product, insurance policies, security, and accessibility. These approvals give traders confidence in elements such as title transfer and quality control, without requiring physical inspection of the goods.

Non-exchange storage offers more flexibility and often costs less, but there is no standardized regulation of these facilities. The risk of utilizing a non-exchange storage facility can often be mitigated by traders conducting their own inspections and regular audits of their goods.

Regardless of facility location or status, storage facilities frequently support logistics operations. Many storage facility operators possess deep knowledge of local customs processes, documentation, and shipping procedures. Some even own or operate transport assets such as trucks, barges, or rail connections. Traders work closely with these operators to ensure the efficient movement of commodities worldwide.

Material that is under the ownership of a trader is known as inventory. This inventory must be safely stored, accurately tracked, and be readily available for redelivery or processing. Storage facilities coordinate with material owners to ensure inventory is handled appropriately and stored securely.

Storage is not a passive component of commodity trading. It requires active monitoring and involvement by the middle and front-office employees to ensure sufficient availability. In April 2020, we witnessed an unprecedented event that demonstrated just how critical storage can be.

As global demand collapsed at the start of the COVID-19 pandemic lockdowns, refineries drastically reduced crude oil processing. Production, however, remained steady initially. Crude continued flowing into storage tanks, pipelines, and even floating vessels, rapidly filling capacity. This was particularly evident at Cushing, Oklahoma, the delivery point for WTI futures.

When the May 2020 futures contract approached expiry, traders holding long positions faced a harsh reality: They would be obligated to take physical delivery of crude that they couldn't store. The other option was to sell their long positions to avoid taking physical delivery.

With no available storage tanks and no buyers of futures contracts, the market dislocated and prices began free-falling. In fact, for a brief time prices actually turned negative, settling at -$37 per barrel on April 20, 2020.

The price decline did not mean WTI crude oil had suddenly lost its intrinsic value. Rather, traders had to pay others to take delivery of crude they could not store themselves. Traders with storage access were able to capture extraordinary profits by taking advantage of the massive spread between the negative May contract and the positive June and July futures contracts.

This crisis reinforced the value of storage in the commodity trading world, not merely as a logistical necessity, but as a key part of the market infrastructure. For physical traders, storage offers flexibility in timing, tax and duty efficiencies, and opportunities to capture profit through spread trades and arbitrage. Storage should always be considered as a strategic asset of trading, not just a logistics expense.

Chapter Summary

- Storage connects production and consumption, allowing traders to manage timing, logistics, and financing efficiently.
- Dry bulk (warehouses, silos) and liquid storage (tank farms) are the two main facility types.
- Facilities often provide value-added services such as blending and sorting.
- Exchange-approved storage facilities ensure standardized quality.
- Non-exchange storage offers greater flexibility and lower cost but requires increased oversight.
- Bonded facilities and FTZs allow for deferred duties and options to re-export duty-free.
- Storage near major ports and hubs minimizes handling costs and increases delivery flexibility.
- The April 2020 WTI crisis demonstrated how storage capacity can directly influence the price of a commodity.
- Successful traders use storage to capture spreads, manage risk, and enhance profitability across evolving market conditions.

Golf, and Knowing When to Keep Quiet

When I started physical trading in the United States, I quickly discovered golf is a second language in the business world. My biggest problem: I was terrible at it.

Golf is not a game of inches or centimeters, it is a game of millimeters. Like trading, golf can be incredibly frustrating and extremely rewarding. Unfortunately for me, it is usually the former. I am often found in a bush on the side of the course, searching for my ball.

The main reason is simple: I just don't put in the hours. I am never at the driving range, working on my short game, or practicing on the putting green.

Expecting to get better at something without putting in the work is a fool's errand. Trading is the same. Hoping to improve at your role or get the opportunity to move up without stepping outside of your comfort zone is just as silly as me expecting to shoot 80 after last week's 104.

Junior employees, particularly new entrants, should behave like sponges absorbing information from each desk they interact with. This doesn't mean working eighty-hour weeks or sacrificing your personal life. But it does mean going out of your way to learn.

Ask questions constantly: *Why do we do it that way? What's the P&L impact?* (there always is one). This is the equivalent of practicing a sport, getting better until the small things seem easy, allowing you to move on to more challenging tasks.

Now, to the second part of the golf-themed lesson.

A trader's ability to remain calm under pressure when millions of dollars are on the line is paramount. Given that, you might expect traders to handle the pressure of a golf course with ease. Not always.

A former colleague of mine is a fantastic golfer and a great trader, but on the golf course he can be a headcase.

During one particular round he was having the game of his life - on track to break 80 for the first time. Knowing his pre-disposition for golf-related mental breakdowns, I barely said a word to him from holes 10 through 16. There was an unspoken acknowledgement that things were going very well.

As he walked to the tee box on the seventeenth hole, our client yells "Hey, you're going to break 80 today - that's incredible"

I looked at my colleague and could see his brain short-circuiting. He promptly shanked the ball and dropped two shots on the hole. *It's OK* I thought to myself, *all he has to do is par the 18th and he still makes it, just everyone stay quiet...*

"That's OK, just part the next one and you can still do it"

He did not par the eighteenth. He did not break 80. And let's just say we scaled back our use of that client's trucking company for a couple of weeks.

Knowing what to say; when to say it; and most important, when to keep quiet are critical skills in physical trading. I've closed many deals and secured meaningful improvements by saying less, not more.

8. Trade Finance and Title Documents

Financing commodities can be relatively simple or it can be incredibly complex, requiring specialized knowledge to ensure companies have sufficient capital to function. A fundamental part of commodity trading is understanding how these commodities are financed because the cost and availability of financing can have a dramatic impact on the profitability of a trade.

Traders rely on lenders to provide liquidity to finance their transactions. Commodity trading is highly cash-intensive and traders look to banks and other lenders to provide the liquidity they need to move goods. In return, banks charge interest, with rates determined by market conditions, the trader's creditworthiness, and the nature of the commodity being traded.

Whether the front office wants to admit it or not, the finance department is just as critical as the trading desk. Without robust financing capabilities, commodity firms would not survive. Finance departments develop relationships with lenders to ensure liquidity remains available.

This chapter is not exhaustive, but it covers the primary methods commodity firms use to finance material.

Before examining specific financing structures, it is essential to understand the concept of a haircut. In finance, a haircut is a reduction applied to the value of the commodity that is being financed.

This reduction creates a risk buffer for the lender. In the event of a default in a collateralized loan, the lender is protected against price fluctuations. Should the lender become the owner of that commodity, they want to be able to sell it without incurring a loss.

The size of the haircut is influenced by several factors including the type of commodity, market liquidity, volatility, location of the goods, and the counterparty's financial strength. More volatile or illiquid commodities attract a larger haircut, while for widely traded, exchange-listed products stored in reputable locations tend to receive lower haircuts. In the case of a haircut being applied, companies will need to cash finance the balance owed to the supplier.

For example, let's say a trader purchases 1,000 mt of refined copper cathode at $10,000/mt. The invoice value for this commodity is $10 million. However, the bank may only lend against 90 percent of that value, applying a 10 percent haircut. That means the bank is financing 90 percent of the commodity or $9 million out of the $10 million value. However, the bank has collateral over 100 percent of the volume of material. The trader's equity finances the remaining 10 percent. Using a bank line, the trader has leveraged their money 10 times.

Revolving Credit Facility (RCF)

The most common method of financing a commodity is a revolving credit facility (RCF). An RCF is a type of loan that allows a company to draw, repay, and redraw funds up to a specified amount during the loan term. The trader does not have to ask the bank to approve each specific transaction in advance.

RCFs are very flexible and companies can borrow funds as needed. They work similarly to a business credit card, but with much higher credit limits.

RCFs may be secured or unsecured. When secured, the lender holds collateral over the underlying commodities of the loan. Should the trading company default, the lender can take ownership of the underlying commodity.

A common structure within an RCF is a borrowing base. A borrowing base is a specific type of RCF which is always secured. The lender will always have ownership of the commodity they are financing should the company default.

Under a borrowing base, the amount a company can draw will be determined by a formula based on the specific value of the goods - for example, the value of the inventory. The company will be required to provide collateral documents in the lender's name to be able to draw from the borrowing base.

Borrowing bases are regularly recalculated based on the value of the underlying collateral. This is important due to the often high volatility of commodity prices. Companies' borrowing capacity must align with both the volume of the product they are trading and the market prices that vary over time.

Both RCFs and borrowing bases can be provided by either a single lender or a group of lenders. A loan that is provided by a group of lenders is known as a syndicated loan. There will often be a lead arranger that organizes the deal and manages the day-to-day relationship with the borrower. Syndicated loans are usually used in larger financing structures where a single lender would not want to bear all the risk.

A key advantage of RCFs and borrowing bases is that once financed, the borrower does not need to request permission from the lender(s) to move material from one location to another, saving them vital time. It also offers flexibility to take advantage of timely spot requests for material that they otherwise would not be able to if they needed to request release of material from the lender first.

In general, the interest rates used in RCFs are variable throughout the loan term, typically calculated against a chosen public benchmark rate plus a fixed spread. For example, 200 basis points above the secured overnight financing rate (SOFR). The 200 points are fixed, but the public benchmark floats, so the interest rate adjusts with the market. Because these facilities are revolving, interest only accrues on the drawn amounts.

Bilateral Finance Lines

Another common form of financing in commodity trading is through a bilateral finance line. Unlike an RCF, which may involve a syndicate of banks and a broad, flexible structure, a bilateral finance line is a one-to-one lending arrangement between a trading company and a single lender.

Bilateral finance lines are typically smaller, simpler, and more tailored to borrower's specific needs than RCFs. While RCFs usually provide wide funding across the business, a bilateral finance line usually finances a narrower set of activities. They are often used to fund short-term working capital requirements or specific flows with a particular producer or consumer.

These facilities can be unsecured or secured depending on the borrower's creditworthiness and the lender's risk appetite. If lines are secured, they will require collateral such as title documents or assignment of receivables. However, unlike borrowing bases which require continuous recalculations of collateral value, bilateral lines often assess collateral only at drawdown.

Bilateral lines are usually quicker to arrange than large-scale RCFs, allowing traders to make rapid decisions on new business. However, a key difference from an RCF is that secured bilateral lines do not usually provide flexibility to move the collateral without the lender's consent. This can add operational delays if not managed proactively, particularly in fast-moving markets where timing is critical.

Bilateral lines are helpful for traders who need additional liquidity beyond their main RCF. These lines can also help diversify their funding base so they are not overly dependent on a single credit facility. A small trader may have between one to five bilateral lines, but a large trader might have dozens across its different business units, products, or jurisdictions.

Cost structures can vary significantly across bilateral lines, reflecting each lender's individual view of the borrower and the specific risks of the financed flows.

Repurchase Agreements

A repurchase agreement (repo) is a collateralized form of financing with stricter rules regarding the movement of material than an RCF or borrowing base. A repo is a sale of the commodity to a lender with a simultaneous agreement to repurchase it in the future. Traders will use repos when material is to be held for known periods. The financing rate under a repo is typically fixed for the duration of the loan, unlike the floating rates used in RCFs.

These repo structures are sometimes used at financial year-ends when companies try to improve their debt ratios by transferring assets and debts off their balance sheets. However, whether inventory financed under a repo can be removed from a company's balance sheet depends on the specific accounting rules the company is using.

When using a repo, the lender controls the commodity until the borrower needs to move or sell the material. At that point, the borrower will repurchase the material from the lender. Banks typically prefer repos, particularly for standardized materials because they have complete control over the commodity, and in the event of a default, they should easily be able to sell it in the market.

At the repo structure's end date, the borrower can either repurchase the commodity at the pre-agreed rates or request to roll to a future date and continue the financing. Given the fluid nature of commodity trading, it is common for repos to be rolled if material is not yet needed for consumption. Buy-back dates can also be brought forward if sales can be made sooner than initially anticipated.

There is a specific type of repo called a hedged repo which works similarly to a regular repo in terms of collateral and control over the material. However, a hedged repo also involves a futures hedge for the financing bank. Hedged repos are commonly used with exchange-deliverable commodities.

At the point of financing the material, the trader will transfer a short futures position to the financing bank in line with the value of the material being financed. Holding the underlying commodity and the short futures position makes it a price-neutral transaction for the bank. If the borrower defaults, the bank has a futures short position it can either deliver the material against (if it is a physically settled futures market), or buy back the futures position when it physically sells the material. A hedged repo typically allows the bank to reduce the haircut on the financing because it is protected against any price volatility. However, the bank may still not finance 100% of the value depending on other factors like type of commodity and location.

<u>Letters of Credit</u>

When a trader wishes to sell to a receiver but is not prepared to take the exposure risk of shipping goods before payment, a common tool used in the industry is a LC. While not technically a financing instrument, LCs are often used in financing trades.

An LC is a payment guarantee issued by a bank on behalf of a buyer that states the bank will pay the supplier once certain conditions have been met. Typically this involves presenting title documents along with other documents such as a certificate of origin, a certificate of analysis, and inspection reports to prove that material is what the supplier is stating.

The conditions around this document presentation are extremely stringent, and even minor errors such as incorrect wording on title documents or grammatical errors like misplaced commas can delay payment by the bank. Companies often have LC experts on their finance desks who scrutinize the title documents and instructions to ensure they are accurate.

Instead of requiring payment at the point of production, LCs can provide a supplier with comfort that payment is secured, allowing sellers to physically ship material before receiving payment from a buyer. An LC shifts the credit risk from the buyer to the bank - provided the seller can provide the correct documents, the bank is obligated to pay for the material.

A standby letter of credit (SBLC) offers a similar guarantee of payment to suppliers, but it is not typically used as the actual form of payment. An SBLC offers the same guarantee of payment as an LC, but it is only drawn upon if a buyer defaults. If that situation arises, the bank will pay the supplier (provided the SBLC terms are met) and then try to reclaim funds from the buyer. Provided the buyer can pay for the material using other financing lines, the SBLC will not be drawn on. It merely acts as an insurance policy in the event it is needed.

Cash Financing

Cash financing is the least preferred method of financing for a commodity trader because it does not leverage the trader's equity. Cash financing does not involve physical cash; it means using company equity instead of a loan. Cash financing carries the highest opportunity cost because it prevents the company from using the liquidity for other ventures.

However, there are some deals where companies have no other option but to finance with cash. It could be that lenders have deemed the region where the transaction is occurring to be too risky to finance. Or the company could not offer the type of collateral a lender needed to provide financing. Sometimes a company may be at capacity for traditional financing lines and need to cash finance individual purchases. Or if negotiations with the bank over financing take too long, a company may use cash to purchase materials initially, then refinance later under a secured loan.

As previously mentioned, most trades involve some cash financing. Even with traditional financing methods, lenders typically do not finance 100 percent of the transaction value. Cash financing will be required to make up the difference or the level of the haircut. Cash financing is also typically required to finance initial and variation margin on futures hedges, unless those trades have been passed over to the bank during the financing period.

Factoring and Discounting

While factoring and discounting aren't used to finance payments for materials, they are closely linked to the financing desk. Both methods can be used to obtain early payment on receivables, thereby reducing the length of time a commodity needs to be financed.

When a company uses factoring, it is selling its receivables to a third party (the factor), typically a bank. The company usually gets paid within a day or two and the factor will charge a fee for this service. The factor takes over the collection of the receivable and, importantly, notifies the customer of the factor's involvement.

Factoring with recourse means that if the customer does not pay, the company that sold the receivables will still owe the factor. Factoring without recourse implies that should the customer default, the factor assumes the risk. While factoring without recourse is more expensive, it reduces counterparty credit risk for the company.

Discounting is similar to factoring in that the company will still be paid before the invoice terms. However, instead of selling the receivable to a bank, the company borrows against the receivable. Under discounting, the company bears all credit risk for the customer's payment performance; however, there is no obligation to inform the customer so discounting offers greater confidentiality than factoring.

Structured Finance

While most commodity companies rely on shorter-term bank facilities to finance daily movement of material, there are times when they want access to longer-dated or larger-scale funding. Structured finance refers to methods of raising capital beyond simple bank loans. These tools are often used to finance strategic initiatives such as expanding trading operations, purchasing assets, or even acquiring companies.

The bond market is one of the most common ways of raising capital. A bond is essentially a long-term IOU. When a company issues a bond, it borrows money from whoever buys it, promising to repay the principal on a specific maturity date, and pay interest. Bonds can be issued with floating or fixed interest rates with terms ranging from a year to over a decade.

By issuing corporate bonds, a trading company can borrow directly from institutional investors, giving it access to large amounts of upfront capital, often at lower costs than shorter-term bank loans. However, how much companies can raise through bonds depends on their credit profile and willingness to provide detailed, ongoing disclosures to investors. Some privately held trading companies may be reluctant to open themselves to that level of public reporting, which limits their use of the bond market.

Title Documents

Title documents sit at the center of commodity trade finance. They provide legal proof of ownership that allows a company to use goods as collateral, secure financing, and initiate payment.

A title document gives the holder ownership over the commodity it references. Understanding what does, and importantly what does not constitute a title document can be the difference between a secure transaction and an extremely risky one. Physical contracts specify exactly which documents must be presented by the seller before payment for the material can be made. The finance desk, and even lenders themselves are heavily involved in crafting contractual language surrounding documentation requirements.

Bill of Lading

The most widely used title document in all of commodity trading, across dry and liquid commodities is the BOL, sometimes shortened to B/L or BL. A BOL not only lists the content of cargo onboard a vessel, but also acts as a binding proof of ownership over those goods.

Every BOL contains a section listing the consignee - the party to whom the bill is made out. When a specific entity is listed as the consignee, that party becomes the legal owner of the goods in transit. Only that entity, or a party to whom it has formally endorsed the BOL, can retrieve the goods from the vessel once it has docked.

However, the consignee can alternatively be made out “to order.” In this case, the BOL becomes a negotiable document: Ownership transfers through possession and endorsement. The holder can endorse it to another party, sometimes multiple times. This structure can facilitate easier trade finance while the cargo is in transit and allows for more fluid onward sales, such as FOB-to-CIF or CIF-to-CIF transactions.

BOLs are (at the time of writing) a physical document, usually printed in sets of three. The holder of the original BOLs can transfer ownership by endorsing them to another counterparty and sending the original BOLs to that party. Once received, that newly endorsed counterparty will assume all legal rights to that material.

In addition to the consignee field, several other sections of the BOL play a critical role in both logistics and trade finance:

- Shipper: Identifies the party delivering the goods to the carrier; banks often check this field when verifying title and performance under letters of credit or other financing structures.
- Notify Party: The party to be informed upon the vessel's arrival; while it does not confer ownership, it is important for coordinating discharge, customs clearance, and onward sales.
- Material Description: Specifies the product, grade, quantity, packaging, and any relevant markings; accuracy is critical because discrepancies between the B/L and the commercial invoice can lead to financing delays, refusal under an LC, or disputes at discharge.
- Freight Paid/Freight Payable (Freight Prepaid vs. Freight Collect): Indicates whether the freight cost has already been settled; this affects a bank's risk assessment as financed cargo typically requires confirmation that freight is prepaid to avoid liens or carrier claims at discharge.
- Date of Issue and On Board Date: Key for determining shipment timing, LC compliance, and eligibility for certain financing periods: Even a one-day variance can result in rejecting a document under strict LC terms. BOL dates are often linked to the QP of a contract so changes to these dates can affect hedging requirements.
- Port of Loading/Port of Discharge: Must match the sales contract and LC terms; any deviation can trigger a compliance issue or require amendments.

For a bank to finance a commodity on a vessel, a BOL is by far the most common title document required. There is often other documentation such as certificates of origin and analysis to prove the quality of material, but these are not title documents - simply additional requirements by the lender.

For a freight forwarding company to retrieve containers or bulk material from a vessel, it must also be holding the original BOLs to prove to the ship owners that it has the right to move material from the dock. Timing in the delivery of BOLs is critical - delays in receiving original BOLs can cause significant delays in unloading, leading to demurrage and detention costs for the material owner.

While other modes of transportation such as trucks, rail, and barges also have BOLs issued, they are not typically considered a title document. Under these circumstances, it will be up to the buyer to negotiate with their financing company exactly how and when these goods are financed.

The ability of traders to access various types of financing, allowing for multiple modes of transport is part of what differentiates them from producers and consumers.

Tank Receipt

For liquid commodities stored in tank farms or terminals, there is no warehouse receipt in the usual dry-bulk sense. Instead, the storage operator issues a tank receipt, also known as a tank warrant, tank certificate, or entitlement certificate.

The tank receipt identifies the commodity grade and specification, volume, facility and tank number, and the party in whose name the inventory is held. A tank receipt functions as a title document similar to a warehouse receipt for metal. However, because liquids in tanks are typically commingled, the receipt represents title to a specified volume of fungible product of an agreed specification, rather than to a specific lot, as is often the case with segregated dry-bulk material.

Pipeline Tickets

Inventory is often transferred through pipelines at major liquid commodity hubs and terminals. A pipeline ticket records the volume of product in the pipeline or delivered into a connected tank in the name of a particular party. Pipeline tickets, together with the terminal's custody-transfer records serve as evidence of title for financing.

Warehouse Receipt

A warehouse receipt is a common title document used for materials stored and financed in a warehouse, such as dry-bulk commodities. Issued by the storage facility, a warehouse receipt details exactly what material is stored, by what company, and where. Once a warehouse receipt has been issued, it can be used as legal proof of ownership. Warehouse receipts are frequently used as collateral in the financing of commodities.

Holding Certificate

Similar to a warehouse receipt is a holding certificate (HC). An HC is a confirmation document that details the inventory of a commodity in a warehouse or other storage location; however, it is not a legally recognized title document. Given their frequent use in the industry, some agreements between buyers and financiers allow for HCs to be used as a title document to pay for the materials. An HC, in addition to a pre-agreed financing structure can give the bank the right to claim goods should they need to. HCs are generally given greater weight when they are issued by a recognized independent third party rather than by a supplier.

Full Release

Another common document in the industry, not a title document but one that will be issued by a warehouse or storage facility, is a full release. A full release is issued to indicate a change in control over physical goods. It allows the named party on the release to collect or instruct further movement of the goods from storage.

Full releases can be sent by the seller to indicate the buyer has paid for the goods, a bank that was previously financing material releasing it back to the buyer, or the owner of the goods releasing them to a logistics provider for further transport. Typically, if full releases are used to pay for a commodity, the buyer will request either an HC or a warehouse receipt after receiving the release.

Conditional Release

One step below a full release is a conditional release. Under a conditional release, the storage facility receives instructions to release the material once certain conditions are met - typically confirmation that goods have been paid for. The most common trigger for a conditional release to become a final release is the buyer sending a Society for Worldwide Interbank Financial Telecommunication (SWIFT) message of their financial transaction to the issuer of the conditional release. SWIFT is a secure, standardized messaging system that banks and other financial institutions use to exchange payment instructions. When a payment is made, the bank will send a SWIFT message confirming that funds have been debited and the payment is being transferred.

Once the issuer of the conditional release has received the necessary confirmation, the seller's permission is no longer needed for full release. This mechanism is less secure than a full release and is still not a title document. However, when materials are being held at a reputable, independent third-party location, particularly one with which a bank has an established relationship, it can be accepted as a payment document to finance material. It is important to note that once conditions are met, release is no longer contingent on instructions from the seller.

Provisional Release

While it is the least secure of the releases, a provisional release still has a place in the industry. A provisional release is a statement from a storage location confirming that goods are being prepared for release, but neither ownership nor control has been transferred yet. It is simply a preliminary step in financing commodities and can provide some confirmation to a bank or buyer that goods actually exist, are being stored at a specific location, and belong to the seller. Similar to conditional releases, the more reputable the storage facility issuing the provisional release, the more weight it will carry.

It is worth noting that while title documents are used throughout the industry to finance and pay for commodities, they are not infallible. There have been multiple cases of fraud involving title documents. Sometimes, fraud is committed through forged or duplicate copies of documents, other times through the misuse of legitimate documents to create the illusion of ownership.

A high-profile example of fraud using a title document is the 2014 metals-warehouse scandal in China, at the port of Qingdao. Duplicate warehouse receipts for copper and aluminum were pledged as collateral to multiple banks and trading firms. When fraud was uncovered, it led to protracted legal battles and losses for several major global banks and traders, costing hundreds of millions of dollars.

Similarly, in 2020, one of Asia's largest oil traders Hin Leong collapsed after pledging the same oil cargoes and inventory to multiple banks as collateral for loans. Tank receipts and inventory statements had been falsified or duplicated, leading lenders to believe they had security over cargoes that either didn't exist, or had already been pledged elsewhere. Estimated losses for the banks exceeded $3 billion.

Incidents like these underscore the need for constant vigilance and rigorous verification when checking and monitoring title documents throughout the trade lifecycle.

Chapter Summary

- Financing is at the core of commodity trading, enabling traders to move large volumes and manage cash-intensive operations.
- Traders use a range of financing methods, from relatively simple RCFs to more complex structured-finance solutions, to maximize liquidity.
- Lenders rarely finance 100 percent of a cargo's value. They apply a haircut to protect against losses in the event of a default.
- Most transactions include an element of cash financing, but traders work to minimize cash usage to preserve liquidity.
- Title documents are essential because they provide proof of ownership and allow for goods to be used as collateral.
- BOLs are the most common title document, used across both dry and liquid commodity trades during vessel transit.
- Tank receipts and pipeline tickets serve as the primary title documents for inland storage and movement of liquid commodities.
- Warehouse receipts issued by approved storage facilities are the principal title documents for dry-bulk commodities.
- While other documents such as holding certificates or releases may also support financing, whether they can be used to finance material payments will depend on the lender's requirements and the reputation of the issuer.
- Traders and lenders must remain vigilant against fraud, as misuse or forgery of title documents has led to large industry losses.

Going the Extra Mile

In this case I went about 800 extra miles, the distance between New York and Atlanta.

I had been working to close a significant amount of business with a customer for some time. In physical trading, the important face-to-face meetings cannot be overstated. However, the customer in question was extremely tough to pin down. I knew that if I could get in front of him for five minutes I'd be able to secure the business.

“What's your schedule like over the next two weeks? I'd love to grab dinner and talk about our proposal.”

“Dinner, ha, I'm flying all across the country without a break. I'll be West Coast, New Orleans, Nashville, St. Louis, then I have to fly internationally and I'm connecting through Atlanta.”

“Atlanta, that's perfect, I actually need to make a trip there for another client so I'll combine. I'll meet you in between your flights for a coffee in arrivals, what time does your flight get you in?”

I did not have another client. I was flying 1600 miles round-trip for a ten-minute airport coffee! But I did not want him heading off to Europe where I knew there was a risk our deal went stale, and he would be sent new offers on a daily basis. I also knew he wouldn't accept the meeting if he thought he was causing me hassle - sometimes a little white lie is necessary.

That ten-minute meeting helped set up the entire book for the next few months.

Trading is not only about taking calculated risks, but also about not letting an opportunity slip because you didn't try everything you could. Whether it is putting in the extra effort to get in front of that busy customer, doing the extra bit of research that puts you ahead of your competitors, or learning something that gives you an edge.

9. Weighing, Sampling, Moisture Determination, and Assaying

Weighing, sampling, moisture determination, and assaying (WSMD) is a pivotal concept across the commodity trading complex. Commodities are frequently traded on a supplier's reputation - buyers will agree to purchase material from a supplier based on past performance and an expected specification. If the results of WSMD fall outside contractual limits, the supplier can face financial penalties. In some cases the buyer may have the right to reject the cargo entirely.

Most commodity contracts are structured to allow buyers to assess the quality and condition of the material before paying for the goods. This process involves four key steps, and while not every commodity requires all four, many do.

Weighing

Ascertaining the weight or volume of a commodity may seem obvious, but commodity contracts are issued in round numbers. A company will buy 1,000 mt of refined metal, or 100,000 barrels of crude oil, or 20,000 bushels of wheat. But in reality, the final amount of a commodity physically delivered will never match the round numbers initially contracted.

Weighing a parcel is required to inform both sides of the trade of the exact quantity for invoicing, hedging, and general inventory planning. The method for calculating the volume will vary by commodity, but a precise value must be determined for both the supplier and the buyer.

Sampling

Every commodity contract will be traded to a specification, whether that's a minimum metallic content, a specific grade of oil, or a classification of coffee bean. To determine the grade or quality of a commodity, a sample must be taken.

Ensuring that samples are taken effectively requires specific knowledge of the commodities being traded. Samples must represent the entire shipment or lot; otherwise the results of any testing will not accurately reflect the parcel's overall quality. Samples must be taken in accordance with the agreed-upon sampling protocols, including frequency, equipment used, and increments taken. Because of these requirements, sampling is performed by independent surveyors or inspectors. Poor sampling is the leading source of disputes in WSMD because even if the lab work performed is perfect, if the sample is not representative, the results can be meaningless.

Moisture Determination

In both liquid and dry-bulk commodity trading, moisture levels are an extremely important factor. Water forms part of most raw materials; its presence is not necessarily detrimental (though in some cases it can be), but it is also not valued. Commodity buyers need to determine the moisture content of the commodity to ensure they are only paying for and hedging the dry commodity content, not the water weight.

Moisture levels can vary dramatically and failing to calculate them accurately can significantly affect profitability.

Assaying

Last but certainly not least is assaying. While sampling is the process of collecting representative material, assaying is the process of analyzing that material to determine its exact chemical composition. Each commodity may have several subcategories of grade, and certain elements or impurities will define the levels at which commodities are bought and sold. It is through assaying that these elements are discovered.

Commodities are traded on an assumption of quality, but it is only through strict analysis that the actual quality of a commodity can be determined. While suppliers frequently provide their own in-house certificates of analysis, third-party inspection companies are widely utilized throughout the industry to provide independent analysis that often governs the final outcomes of a physical commodity contract.

Let's look at a copper concentrates parcel of 10,000 wet metric tons (WMT). WMT means the volume includes the moisture content of this parcel. A concentrate parcel will have an assumed moisture level, metallic content, and payable percentage. Payable percentages are linked to the recovery rate when processing the raw material.

Someone unfamiliar with WSMD may think the payment and exposure is on the gross 10,000 WMT. But as discussed, a company will only pay for and hedge the actual payable volume. In the case of concentrates, this is the dry (removing moisture), metallic, payable content.

For this parcel, let's assume an 8 percent moisture level, a 25 percent copper content, and a 96.5 percent payable. The following example illustrates how each step in WSMD affects the final payable and hedgeable tonnage:

- 10,000 * 92% = 9,200 Dry Metric Tons (DMT)
- 9,200 * 25% = 2,300 Metallic Contained Tons
- 2,300 * 96.5% = 2,219.50 Payable Tons

For payment, the company will only pay for 2,219.50 mt. For hedging purposes, to the nearest lot on the LME this would be 2,225 mt or 89 lots. If this were pricing on the Chicago Mercantile Exchange (CME) it would be 4,900,000 lbs or 196 lots.

However, these initial calculations are typically made on provisional assays provided by the supplier. It is not until the final WSMD has taken place that the definitive numbers will be known.

Once the material is ready for shipment at the port or warehouse, it will be moved to a conveyor belt for loading onto a vessel. The trucks will be weighed both light (empty) and heavy (loaded) to determine the weight. Some conveyor belts have certified scales built into the belt itself to determine weight. Inspectors are often present at weighing to prevent disputes arising over volume at a later stage.

Samples will be taken at the contractually specified location to ensure a fair representation across the entire 10,000 WMT parcel. These samples will be sent to the inspector's laboratory for detailed testing for any chemical elements contained within the contract, along with moisture levels.

The buyer and seller will then use the WSMD results to finalize the contract.

When trading commodities, even small shifts from provisional analysis to final analysis can have significant impacts. For the above copper concentrate parcel, the buyer assumed a copper content of 25 percent. If after receiving the final analysis, the actual copper content was 24.5 percent, that would mean the correct payable tonnage is 2,175.11MT, and the correct hedgeable tonnage is 2,175 mt or 87 lots. If the buyer had already hedged this parcel, they would be over-hedged by two lots. It doesn't take long for a 50 mt copper exposure to become very costly.

This is why WSMD departments work hand in hand with operations and risk desks to ensure that any exposures are mitigated quickly.

Understanding the nuances of WSMD can be the difference between profit and loss, and sometimes between a long career in commodities and a short one.

Chapter Summary

- WSMD underpins most physical commodity contracts, ensuring the correct weight, quality, and payables are established before final settlement.
- Weighing determines the actual quantity delivered, which is rarely the same as the contracted round number.
- Sampling accuracy is critical. If samples are not representative of the entire cargo, analysis can be meaningless.
- Moisture determination adjusts quantities to account for water weight, so buyers only pay for the commodity itself.
- Assaying provides a definitive chemical composition, which drives pricing, payables, and penalties.
- Discrepancies between provisional and final WSMD results can materially affect invoicing and risk positions, requiring efficient management and collaboration between WSMD and operations, risk, and finance teams.
- All elements of the WSMD procedure should be contractually agreed to avoid disputes over protocols.

Mexico

Tropical water, white sands, and margaritas are what many people think of when they picture traveling to Mexico. My first time in this amazing country looked slightly different from sipping drinks in Cancun.

Landing in Mexico City is an experience. Flying over mountainous terrain to suddenly see a city of 22 million people appear out of nowhere still surprises me. The airport itself is in the middle of the city - which is uncommon for major international airports. There is always a part of me that thinks we're going to clip buildings on approach.

To trade lead in North America, you need to have a handle on the Mexican landscape. A large portion of the lead imported to the United States comes from Mexico, so a tour had been organized for me to meet the producers. This involved a short stay in Mexico City, followed by flying around Mexico - Monterrey, San Luis Potosi, and Chihuahua.

As we landed at the Monterrey Regional Airport, I was taken aback by the car that picked us up. To say it could use a tune-up was an understatement. I could sense my boss was thinking the same thing, which our guide immediately noticed. "If I picked you up in an Escalade, we wouldn't make it to our destination, bandits everywhere."

I knew we were in safe hands but it was still a bit unnerving, and occasionally the local trader from the Mexico office would shout "*Rápido!*" at the driver. I don't speak Spanish but I know enough to understand that does not mean "take your time."

Fortunately the trip was largely uneventful; at each stop we were greeted enthusiastically, and every supplier genuinely appreciated the effort required to come and meet in person.

And I got to sample a local delicacy known as *escamoles*. The locals ordered for us, and I'll let you research to see what they contain, but I needed a few tequilas to wash them down.

Commodity trading will take you to places far removed from conference rooms and video calls. Sometimes you'll travel by plane and sometimes by rickety cars held together by duct tape and hope. But showing up in person matters; it builds trust in ways an email or phone call never can.

10. Mark-to-Markets, P&Ls, and Reporting

An unavoidable part of commodity trading, regardless of department, is the constant monitoring and reporting of company profits and exposures. Senior management tracks each trading book's performance. Individual traders want to ensure their positions are performing as expected. Operations ensure that invoices are paid and properly allocated. Finance and accounting teams liquidate contracts as they progress through the trade life cycle.

Because of this monitoring there is a huge focus on the accuracy and methods of reporting that companies use.

Most physical commodity deals reflect at least a multi-month period, and yearly contracts are commonly booked. It is not uncommon for some offtake or supply agreements to be contracted for multi-year periods. The reason is that end consumers need to guarantee a consistent supply of resources. While consumers may leave some volumes open to accommodate disruptions, a base level of supply will be booked to ensure business continuity.

This means that a trader who books a sales contract in Q4 of 2025 to supply a commodity on a monthly basis throughout 2026 will not liquidate portions of that contract for over a year after booking. That is a long time for a company to wait to reflect the expected results of that deal in its financial statements. This is where mark-to-market accounting comes into play.

Mark-to-Market

Mark-to-market (MTM) is an accounting method that allows businesses to recognize unrealized gains or losses at the inception of a deal, rather than waiting until the contract is physically completed or liquidated. Before MTM usage, companies could only book profit from trades as the physical cargo was invoiced.

MTM valuations use prevailing prices, benchmarks, and contract values to produce an accurate profit or loss report after a trade is booked. While changes to physical contracts are common as deals move through their life cycle, a MTM will provide an inception P&L and immediately capture any changes in costs from that point on.

For example, a trader buys 10,000 mt of refined aluminum at a premium of $300/mt, to be delivered over the following six months. The trader's expected additional costs (to move the metal to an end consumer sale) at the time of purchase are $50/mt. The company hedges the outright price risk of the metal, so price changes will not affect the trade's profits.

At the time of agreeing the purchase, the benchmark premium for this material is $400/mt. Therefore, the initial profit calculation is as follows:

- Benchmark premium: $400/mt
- Total costs: $350/mt ($300/mt purchase premium + $50/mt costs)
- Profit at time of purchase: $50/mt * 10,000 mt, or $500,000 total

Even though the company has not taken delivery of the purchase, and may not have a physical sale booked, this profit can be recognized immediately.

Looking at an agricultural market, a trader agrees to sell 1,000,000 bushels of corn at $0.80/bushel over the Chicago Board of Trade (CBOT) futures price, FOB Gulf. In corn, the premium is known as "basis." The CBOT futures price plus the basis price equals the cash price.

If at the time of the sale, the benchmark basis for corn FOB Gulf is $0.78/bushel, the initial profit calculation is as follows:

- Benchmark basis: $0.78/bushel
- Sale basis: $0.80/bushel
- Profit at time of sale: $0.02/bushel * 1,000,000 bushels, or $20,000 total

If in the corn example the trader did not hedge their outright price risk, the

MTM would factor the current exchange price of corn into profit levels.

Let's say the sale was made at a CBOT price of $4.3725/bushel plus the basis of $0.80/bushel. That would give a sale price of $5.1725/bushel. If the CBOT price remained unchanged, the MTM would still reflect the $0.02/bushel profit. However, if the CBOT futures price decreased from the point of agreeing the sale, the MTM would increase from the original $20,000 level because the trader could buy corn at a lower CBOT price than its sale:

- Sale price: $5.1725/bushel
- Benchmark basis: $0.78/bushel
- CBOT futures price: $4.2725
- MTM **profit**: $0.12/bushel * 1,000,000 bushels, or $120,000 total

However, if the CBOT futures price increased then the MTM would decrease accordingly because the trader would have to pay a higher CBOT price than its sale:

- Sale Price: $5.1725/bushel
- Market Purchase basis: $0.78/bushel
- CBOT futures price: $4.4750
- MTM **loss**: $0.0825/bushel * 1,000,000 bushels, or $82,500 total

In a scenario where the outright price risk is not, or cannot be hedged, the MTM will continue to change with the underlying price of the commodity until the trader's position is flat (neither long nor short physical). This is why most traders hedge their outright price risk whenever possible so their physical profits are not affected by changes in the commodity price.

Accurate MTMs depend on using reliable market benchmarks. Benchmarks are reference values used to assess the current fair value of a trade. In commodities, these benchmarks could include exchange-based premiums or discounts, treatment and refining charges, or percentage payables. These dynamic benchmarks allow companies to update the value of their positions in real-time, even without a physical invoice or sale. Actual premiums or discounts vary by commodity, location, logistics, quality, and timing.

As market benchmarks continue to oscillate, the value of each trade on the books will also change. If in the aluminum example, the benchmark sale premium rises by $50/mt, the MTM would increase by $50/mt on any remaining tonnage yet to be invoiced from the 10,000 mt purchase. If the benchmark sale premium decreased by $50/mt, the MTM would decrease by $50/mt on any remaining tonnage.

A well managed MTM will continuously capture changes in premiums, discounts, treatment charges, payables, expected or known logistics costs, finance and credit costs, hedging gains and losses, among a host of other factors. To ensure accuracy, it is vital that as soon as changes to these benchmarks or expenses are known, the physical contracts are updated accordingly. A MTM is only as good as the information it receives. If the trading system does not capture contract costs, the MTM will not accurately reflect the company's profits.

MTMs serve a dual purpose: financial reporting and internal risk control. From a reporting standpoint, they provide a daily snapshot of a company's economic health. Without running an updated MTM, companies may be blind to changes in benchmarks or costs until working through P&Ls at the end of each month.

Sudden changes in MTM values can also highlight data-entry errors, mispriced contracts, or unexpected market shifts. It enables companies to take a proactive response to these risks, rather than reactive corrections after contract liquidation.

Management of MTMs is not always a front-office task. A large amount of the information reported in the MTM stems from the middle-office. Being aware of any changes to the MTM can alert the middle-office to mistakes, both in input and in the system itself. Also, if someone makes a change to a contract that should have resulted in a MTM change but did not see one, it is equally important to raise a question. Errors identified quickly can usually be dealt with quickly and at minimal cost. The longer it takes to identify an error, the larger the potential loss.

MTMs used to capture changes not only in physical trading P&Ls but also in derivative trading.

Executed futures contracts will receive a daily valuation from the point of execution - this is essentially the same as a variation margin. Contracts will be valued against the settlement price for that commodity daily, and the profit or loss will be reflected in the MTM.

For example, if a derivatives trader went long (bought) 100 NYMEX WTI crude oil futures contracts (each representing 1,000 barrels) at $75/bbl, and the following day's settlement price for that prompt month rose to $77/bbl, the MTM would reflect a gain of $2/bbl or $200,000. If the following day's settlement decreased to $73/bbl, the MTM would reflect a loss of $2/bbl or $200,000.

Whether the futures contracts were executed for hedging purposes or for speculative trading, the gain would be reflected in the MTM in the same way. Once any open futures positions have been closed, the MTM will no longer be affected by further price movements because there is no remaining futures exposure.

Even when using MTM accounting, companies may still have employees go through the P&Ls at the end of each month to ensure that the figures reported in the MTM are accurate.

The requirements for reporting will vary depending on whether a company is public or private and on the jurisdiction in which it operates. However, even privately held commodity traders will engage an external auditor at least once a year to assess their profitability. The auditors will analyze benchmarks to ensure that the numbers the company is using to establish its MTM are accurate. Companies that do not provide audited financials will struggle to achieve financing or obtain credit lines to conduct their business.

When appropriately used, MTM accounting is a perfectly acceptable and efficient way to report financial information. However, like most systems it can be abused. Companies rely on their trading staff to honestly capture current market conditions and expected costs. A trader who books a big business just before the financial year end (coinciding with bonus time), may be tempted to inflate the MTM, either by deliberately not entering known costs or using a benchmark that is not reflective of the market. Most companies will not wait for auditors to catch errors; they will have safeguards in place to prevent traders from misusing the system.

The most famous example of MTM accounting abuse is Enron. From 1985 until its eventual collapse in 2001, Enron was viewed as one of the world's largest physical energy traders. It relied on large, multi-year contracts for headline profits, but its switch to MTM accounting enabled it to book exaggerated forward earnings and conceal weak underlying performance.

Enron's traders were able to make huge forward profits on projects that were unlikely to deliver those returns. Those inside Enron knew that profits were inflated, but as long as MTM values stayed positive, reported earnings and the share price continued to rise.

By the time the scope of fraud was uncovered it was too late. In December 2001 Enron filed for Chapter 11 bankruptcy, leading to the loss of thousands of jobs. The scandal led to increased calls for corporate accountability and was a catalyst for the Sarbanes-Oxley Act of 2002, which aimed to improve corporate governance and financial oversight. Unsurprisingly, Arthur Andersen - the accounting firm that audited Enron - also collapsed and was forced out of business because of its involvement in the scandal.

Chapter Summary

- Commodity contracts often span months or years, requiring ongoing valuation before final delivery.
- MTM accounting enables early recognition of P&L, providing a daily snapshot of the value of company positions.
- Accurate reporting of benchmarks and costs is essential because outdated or incorrect data distorts reported profits.
- Hedging helps to isolate costs from outright price, stabilizing the MTM.
- Close collaboration between front, middle, and back-office teams is required to improve MTM accuracy and spot errors, omissions, and unexpected MTM swings early.
- Auditors and strong corporate governance reinforce trust in the figures reported to stakeholders.

NASCAR Close-Up

I had just booked a sizable business with a battery producer and to celebrate they had invited me to a NASCAR event. They were both sponsors and battery providers for one of the race teams. For those unfamiliar, NASCAR involves driving extremely high-powered cars around an oval-shaped track, anywhere from 200 to 500 laps at frightening speeds.

The event was held in Bristol, Tennessee. Bristol is a tiny regional airport that you cannot fly to directly from New York, so I connected through Charlotte, North Carolina. As I approached the gate for the final leg, I was asked to step onto a scale. Not my luggage - me. As mentioned, I am not a comfortable flyer, so learning that the flight's safety potentially depended on how much I weighed did not put me at ease.

Upon landing in Bristol, I could not have imagined the sheer scale of this event. The entire town had been transformed into a NASCAR village. There were campsites, food vendors, and merchandise stalls for miles around the stadium. I even saw a motorhome that was transporting a sports car in the luggage bay so the owners could cruise around the event in style.

I met my client who handed me my pass, granting us access to the track itself. We had great seats in a box overlooking the middle of the circuit. This turned out to be crucially important if we wanted to hold a conversation. Stepping out into the raceway I was instantly deafened. The sound of the engines was comparable to a jet taking off. You cannot hear a thing, and yet the capacity crowd of 146,000 seemed blissfully unfazed. Everyone eagerly watched, waiting for the next overtaking maneuver; pitstop; or, let's be honest, crash.

Trackside viewing really allowed for a different experience. You could feel the track vibrate beneath your feet from the power of the cars. The reaction times of the drivers as they raced at speeds exceeding 200 miles per hour - avoiding debris and other cars while listening to instructions over the radio - was something to behold.

As traders we must navigate high-pressure environments, but this was something different. One wrong move, a second late on a gear change, breaking too early or too late, these guys were heading into a steel barrier. The margin for error was microscopic.

Sometimes a trip can give you a much-needed new perspective on how to deal with stressful situations, and this was one of those times. The earplugs we wore to avoid permanent hearing damage forced me to observe rather than talk - picking up on details that would likely have gone unnoticed from the quiet comfort of our box seats.

The best traders learn how to turn down the noise and read the situation calmly, quietly, and with precision.

11. Futures Exchanges and Hedging

While it is not a prerequisite to understand the details of how commodity exchanges function, having a base level knowledge enhances one's understanding of why and how commodities trade the way they do.

Futures Exchanges

Commodity futures exchanges evolved from the need to reduce price uncertainty. Grain merchants wanted a way to lock in prices before they harvested crops. Metal merchants wanted to establish prices before materials sailed on three-month voyages.

Before exchanges were established, commodity price discovery was fragmented and opaque. Moving price discovery onto an exchange improved transparency and provided traders with publicly available reference prices for their trades.

The first recognized, organized commodity exchange is widely credited as the Dojima Rice Exchange, founded in Osaka, Japan in 1697. It featured standardized contracts for rice and established futures contracts in the form of rice tickets that could be held for future physical delivery.

One of the most famous commodity exchanges is the Chicago Board of Trade (CBOT), founded by grain merchants in 1848, which has made Chicago a global center for agricultural trading. The CBOT merged with the Chicago Mercantile Exchange (CME) in 2007. The New York Cotton Exchange and New York Mercantile Exchange (NYMEX), established in the 1870s, traded cotton, butter, and cheese before expanding into other products such as energy and metals. In 2008 the CME acquired NYMEX, bringing energy and metals under its umbrella.

The largest exchange for metals is the LME, founded in 1877 to facilitate standardized physical trading of industrial metals such as copper and tin.

Today, most commodities traded globally have a futures exchange where price discovery occurs. By concentrating bids and offers from around the world into one venue, exchanges produce a transparent price that reflects the market's collective view of supply and demand.

Exchange prices serve as the benchmark for the physical contracts that trade these commodities. Whether a company is shipping refined metal from Europe to China, crude oil from the Middle East to the United States, or cotton from Brazil to India, there is a fair, public mechanism for setting the price of their contracts. Exchanges also offer futures contracts that allow traders to hedge against or speculate on price movements.

It is worth noting that a futures exchange does not have to exist for a commodity to trade - there are commodities for which prices for physical contracts are still set in private deals or using price reporting agencies. But where a futures exchange exists, it usually becomes the global benchmark.

Futures on commodity exchanges are standardized contracts. Each futures contract that trades will have a defined volume, for example 25 mt of copper cathode per contract on the LME, or 1,000 barrels of crude oil on the Intercontinental Exchange (ICE).

Contracts will also reference specific qualities or grades of a commodity. This standardization enables the highest liquidity and gives traders the confidence to enter and exit positions without negotiating bespoke terms for each trade.

A futures contract is an agreement to buy or sell a specific tonnage of a commodity at an agreed price, at a specific date in the future. Once entered into it becomes an obligation that will settle on the date agreed in the contract. Depending on the commodity, this date can be as near as the following day, or months or even years in the future.

Unlike equity exchanges, commodity futures can settle physically. If an exchange futures contract is physically settled, a short futures position if left open and held to expiry, will become a physical obligation to deliver that commodity in the volume of the futures contract, to an exchange-approved storage location.

A long futures position, if left open and taken to expiry, will become a physical obligation to pay for and take delivery of that commodity in the volume of the futures contract, at an exchange approved storage location.

Most of the time traders do not use the exchanges for this function so careful management of open futures positions is required. But occasionally, traders will utilize the exchanges as either a supply source, or a delivery point for the commodities they trade.

Most major commodities have a few dominant futures exchanges that set the reference price:

Nonferrous metals: LME, CME, Shanghai Futures Exchange (SHFE)
Ferrous metals: Singapore Exchange (SGX), Dalian Commodity Exchange (DCE), CME, LME
Energy: ICE, NYMEX, Shanghai International Energy Exchange (INE)
Agriculture: Zhengzhou Commodity Exchange (ZCE), DCE, CME, ICE

Producers, consumers, and traders rely on these exchange prices to value inventories, negotiate contracts, and manage exposures.

Hedging

Although some physical traders do utilize futures exchanges to speculate on commodity price direction, the majority of physical traders use exchanges to hedge their outright price exposures for the underlying commodities they trade.

The transparency of commodity exchanges means that traders are not in control of commodity prices. Because of this, prices can shift significantly between agreeing on the price of a physical purchase and sale. Traders that do not mitigate this are taking a massive risk with the profitability of their physical trades.

Not hedging is akin to playing roulette in a casino. You may bet on red and get lucky, landing on a string of eight reds in a row, but the next spin will land on black, and the losses could be enough to wipe out your entire profits. Commodity prices are the same - you may get lucky for a few trades in a row, but when the price moves against you the losses on that one trade could erase an entire month's or even a year's profits. Even very successful derivative traders are often incorrect about the outright direction of price movements.

Hedging allows traders to become price agnostic. As much as we'd like to think (hope) prices will move the way we want, this is not the case. Once a company has executed a hedge correctly, its profits will not be affected by any subsequent price moves.

A hedge is an equal-and-opposite futures position relative to the physical commodity transaction. If a trader fixes the price of a physical purchase, the hedge would be to sell futures. If fixing the price of a physical sale, the hedge would be to buy futures. Importantly, the hedge should be executed at the same time the physical price is agreed.

For example, if a trader were buying 100mt of Robusta coffee (traded on the ICE Europe exchange) at a price of $4,000/mt, it would at the same time sell 100 mt Robusta coffee futures (10 futures contracts) at a price of $4,000/mt.

Let's say the trader sells the 100 mt of physical coffee a few days later at a price of $3,900/mt. At the same time as agreeing the physical sale price, the trader would buy 100mt of Robusta coffee futures at a price of $3,900/mt, as shown in Table 1.

Table 1

	mt	Price $/mt	Cash Flow
Physical Purchase	100	$ 4,000	$ (400,000.00)
Futures Sale	-100	$ 4,000	$ 400,000.00
Physical Sale	-100	$ 3,900	$ 390,000.00
Futures Purchase	100	$ 3,900	$ (390,000.00)
	0		**$ -**

In this example, the price of coffee decreased between the physical purchase and sale. However, the trader's futures hedge protected it against the price drop.

Looking at these transactions another way, the trader is losing $100/mt or $10,000 between its physical purchase and sale. However, it is gaining the exact same $100/mt or $10,000 from the price difference between its futures sale and purchase, as shown in Table 2.

Table 2

	mt	Price $/mt	Cash Flow
Physical Purchase	100	$ 4,000	$ (400,000.00)
Physical Sale	-100	$ 3,900	$ 390,000.00
Physical Totals	**0**		**$ (10,000.00)**
Futures Sale	-100	$ 4,000	$ 400,000.00
Futures Purchase	100	$ 3,900	$ (390,000.00)
Futures Totals	**0**		**$10,000.00**
Overall Position	**0**		**$ -**

If the company had not hedged in this scenario, it would have faced an outright loss of $10,000 - the difference between the physical purchase and sale price.

Conversely, if the price increases between a physical purchase and sale, hedging prevents a company from profiting from that price increase. But the point here is that companies do not know which direction, or by how much commodity prices will move between fixing the prices of their physical positions. Companies cannot afford to take risk prices moving in their favor, so hedging is the logical choice to ensure long-term profitability.

Commodities typically trade at a premium, a discount, or a percentage of the exchange price. Hedging allows companies to isolate their profit or loss from the differences in premiums, discounts, or percentages at which they buy and sell their physical commodities.

In the above example, let's say the trader had bought the 100mt of coffee at an FOB Ho Chi Minh City (Vietnam is by far the largest Robusta exporter) at a premium of $80/mt, and sold it CIF Antwerp (Europe's main coffee import hub) at a premium of $250/mt. If it had an ocean freight cost of $120/mt, with finance costs of $10/mt and insurance costs of $2/mt, it would show a gross profit on the trade of $38/mt as shown in Table 3.

Table 3

	mt	Price $/mt	Premium	Ocean Freight	Vessel Insurance	Finance Cost	Cash Flow
Physical Purchase	100	$ 4,000	$ 80	$ 120	$ 2	$ 10	$ (421,200.00)
Futures Sale	-100	$ 4,000	-	-	-	-	$ 400,000.00
Physical Sale	-100	$ 3,900	$ 250	-	-	-	$ 415,000.00
Futures Purchase	100	$ 3,900	-	-	-	-	$ (390,000.00)
	0						**$ 3,800.00**

Despite the price decreasing by $100/mt, the trader's $38/mt profit or $3,800 is secured by the hedging it executed. In physical commodity trading, profits come not from betting on the flat price, but from capturing and managing the premiums and discounts to the exchange price, while using futures to neutralize outright price risk.

Chapter Summary

- Commodity exchanges were created to reduce uncertainty over commodity prices and bring transparency to previously opaque markets.
- Exchange prices serve as public reference points for valuing physical commodity trades worldwide.
- Futures contracts are standardized for each commodity across volume, quality, and settlement dates, enabling high liquidity.
- Some commodity futures contracts can be physically settled by delivering or taking delivery of the commodity at an exchange-approved location.
- Futures exchanges do not exist for every commodity traded globally - these commodities are priced privately or through price-reporting agencies.
- Physical commodities often trade at a premium or a discount to the exchange price to reflect origin, quality, logistics, and timing.
- Traders use futures contracts to hedge against fluctuations in the underlying price of physical commodities.
- If physical trades were left unhedged, profits would be exposed to price movements outside of the traders' control.
- Hedging allows traders to become price-agnostic, with margins produced from differences in premiums and discounts rather than betting on price direction.

Rolling Around in Rwanda

Building a book is far more complicated than taking one over. An established book still requires careful management, but you have a base to build upon. Building something from scratch is daunting, but if you can get it off the ground you have complete ownership of the profits.

This was the task ahead of Tom. As a young trader he was keen to prove himself. Building a tin metal book in sub-Saharan Africa screamed opportunity. If he was successful, he knew there would be further opportunities, perhaps a little closer to home.

So, after acclimatizing to his new role, and life for now, Tom set about the difficult task of sourcing. Sales would not be a problem; he had a global network to rely on.

A lot of the mining in Africa is described as "artisanal." In the West, this is a term we give to bakeries when we justify paying over the odds for a locally baked loaf of bread. In Africa, it means there are many small, privately operated production sites rather than large, industrial facilities. Major, well-established mines have no problem marketing their production. The real opportunity was in developing relationships with the smaller producers.

However, this opportunity presents a challenge from both an ESG and operational standpoint. Vetting small miners for environmental and labor standards, tracing material origin, confirming no child labor, and physically accessing remote sites to validate volumes. Tom frequently had to navigate dirt roads, sometimes no roads at all, to reach production and negotiate contracts.

On one such trip, Tom was driving his Jeep through rural Rwanda when at the last second he saw a crater in the road large enough to swallow the front axle. He swerved, avoiding the hole but could not keep all four tires on the road. The car began to tip, quickly reaching a point where it turned into a full on roll. After three complete rotations the car came to a rest. Tom, highly thankful for the rollbars and his seatbelt, crawled out of the car with only a few scratches.

It's hard to account for every single risk in a trade, or in this case every single pothole in a road. But the mitigation we put in place, whether through planning, hedging, or simply wearing a seatbelt, can be the difference between profit and loss, and sometimes life and death.

12. Compliance, ESG, and Ethics in Commodities

For decades, much of the commodities industry was viewed as a "Wild West," where contracts were obscured from public view, companies played by their own rules, and oversight was negligible at best.

This reputation was compounded further by the actions of the "father of modern commodities trading" - Marc Rich. While Rich can be credited for creating the spot market for crude oil, he was also indicted on federal charges for tax evasion, racketeering, and illegal trading with Iran during the hostage crisis. Those who learned from him and went on to form some of the largest commodity trading companies in the world, were often far too aggressive in pursuing business by any means.

However, Glencore's IPO in 2011 and subsequent merger with Xstrata thrust commodity trading into the public sphere like never before. While opportunities expanded, so did scrutiny - not only of trading companies but also of their lenders. Even privately held trading companies still relied heavily on large, public banks that could not afford to be caught up in controversy.

Until the late 2010s, ESG issues were widely seen as marketing spin. But over the past decade, the public has become increasingly aware that without improvements in how commodities are sourced and converted, we risk irreversible damage to the planet and devastating consequences for communities.

Among the large trading houses, producers, and consumers, you would be hard-pressed to find one that has not had a negative encounter with an ESG or ethics issue. Some, such as oil spills or bribery cases, are highly publicized. Others have stayed hidden behind closed doors. But in 2025, any incident that runs afoul of public perception quickly becomes a major business risk.

In the past, the public often pretended not to notice. Today, whether the perceived consequences materialize or not, consumers are now actively voting with their wallets. Companies that fail to respond to public pressure risk boycotts and rapidly shrinking profits. Some call it "cancel culture," and others call it the free market.

Access to financing has become a critical ESG driver. Banks, many of them publicly owned, are changing their priorities. They are demanding documented ESG policies from companies before extending credit. The last thing a bank wants is to be tied to a deal that ends up involving pollution or child labor. Whether the bank was complicit or not does not matter - they will be tarred with the same brush as the trader if things go wrong.

This is not just about trading companies. To obtain financing for new mining projects, drilling capacity, pipelines, ship-building, and virtually any new project, banks now demand evidence of how environmental and social risks will be mitigated. Without it, securing financing is increasingly challenging.

Governments are not immune to this pressure either. In democracies, politics is ultimately a popularity contest. Younger generations, who are more environmentally conscious and politically active, are demanding stricter environmental and social standards. As a result, regulations are tightening worldwide. To operate in many countries, companies must comply. Given the global nature of commodity markets, every trader, large or small, is exposed to these policies.

Several industries are considering an entirely different pricing model for commodities produced using “green” techniques versus those made with older technology. Green premiums in metals such as copper, aluminum, steel, and nickel, where production involves lower carbon footprints are starting to trade at higher prices. ESG is not just cost avoidance; it is a profit driver.

Insurance companies are also following banks’ lead. Cargoes, vessels, or projects that do not meet ESG criteria face considerably higher premiums or sometimes outright refusal of cover. Without the ability to insure cargoes, trading becomes impossible.

ESG is also a top concern among new and prospective employees at trading firms, whereas in the past it may have been at the bottom of the list. The newest generation of employees cares deeply about these issues, and to attract the best talent, companies must demonstrate a genuine commitment to ESG. Those that fail to do so risk losing the next wave of leaders to competitors that take ESG seriously.

However, ESG is not just about climate. Companies are spending millions on anti-bribery, anti-money laundering, and anti-corruption training. When I began my career in 2009, there was no ESG department. My anti-bribery training consisted of clicking through an e-book with the gist being "don't take or give money in a suitcase." Today, training involves interactive workshops, policy creation, and regular reviews - all stemming from senior management.

Companies are also conducting far deeper KYC procedures, not merely analyzing the counterparty's financial health but also scrutinizing the ethical behavior of owners and employees. Similar to banks, traders do not want to get caught up buying from or selling to a company that might tarnish their reputation by association.

It does not stop at personal behavior either; companies are increasingly using technology to verify complete supply chains. IoT sensors gathering real-time environmental data, blockchain tracking, and satellite imagery are all being used to prove everything from ethical cobalt sourcing and deforestation-free palm oil to vessel emissions monitoring.

The cynic may say that traders are simply following the guidelines to prevent a PR backlash. But in reality, the leading companies recognize the benefits of these policies and see them as a way to strengthen their business and improve industry standards.

It is not enough to have ESG policies and strict corporate governance; companies must prove they are real. ESG audits, emissions reporting, and third-party certifications are now standard practice to avoid being accused of greenwashing. Companies that talk a big ESG game without implementing policy can face both reputational and legal damage, often worse than ignoring ESG altogether.

Failure to meet ESG standards is not merely a PR issue; it is increasingly leading to lawsuits, fines, and even bans in specific markets. For example, the EU Corporate Sustainability Reporting Directive (CSRD) and the forthcoming Corporate Sustainability Due Diligence Directive (CSDDD) will make companies legally liable for human rights and environmental abuses in their supply chains.

Even the notoriously neutral Switzerland, home to some of the largest commodity traders in the world, has faced pressure to move away from self-regulation and implement a more robust framework to address concerns over sanctions enforcement and the potential for corruption.

Countries are increasingly working together on cross-border investigations, expanding the scope and reach of regulators who have to probe the inner workings of commodity trading firms.

In 2025, ignoring ESG can cause more than reputational damage. From financing and insurance, to talent retention and consumer pressure, failures in ESG policy can mean losing access to markets altogether.

Chapter Summary

- For a long time, the commodity business operated as a 'Wild West', with limited oversight and tolerance for aggressive, sometimes illegal practices.
- Today, commodity traders are in the public spotlight, creating the need for transparency and accountability.
- ESG policy shifted from being a PR tactic to a core driver of business, shaping the landscape of financing, insurance, permitting, recruitment, and even creating new 'green' industries within commodities.
- Public and governmental pressures penalize firms seen as unethical or environmentally harmful.
- Regulators globally have tightened rules to make firms liable for abuses in their supply chains.
- Historical scandals illustrate the stakes with ESG breaches leading to fines in the hundreds of millions of dollars.
- Leading companies increasingly view ESG policies not as a burden but as a competitive edge, attracting investors, employees, and counterparties willing to pay a premium for responsibly sourced commodities.

Attention to Detail

It's one of those clichés people list under "strengths" on a resume, then never think about again. But in commodity trading, attention to detail can be the difference between saving the day and losing six figures.

A couple of months into my first role as an operator, I was tasked with arranging a payment for ocean freight. Nothing complicated, just EUR 975.00 to a small shipping company in an obscure country. A routine admin task you could do half-asleep.

For this particular contract, we had to send proof of freight payment to our supplier, so I requested the SWIFT confirmation from treasury. Typically you wouldn't look twice at a SWIFT; it's just a confirmation showing the payment went through. But that day, for reasons I still can't explain, I gave it a second look.

And that's when my stomach dropped. In the value box, it didn't say EUR 975.00; it said EUR 975,000. We had just paid one thousand times too much for a short sea freight booking to an obscure freight company.

My first thought was that I must have entered something wrong, so I double-checked the payment order. It was correct. The system had misread the value. Panicking, I ran to my manager, who looked at it, smiled grimly, and said, "Ah. You've just learned the European decimal rule."

In many European countries, a comma is used as the decimal separator and a period as the thousands separator. What I entered as "EUR 975.00" was interpreted as "EUR 975,000."

Fortunately, we managed to contact the bank quickly enough to reverse the payment, but those were some of the longest hours of my early career. After that, the payment procedure was changed to require the amount to be written out in full, the same way you'd write a check. (For anyone under twenty-five: checks are a way to pay people using paper. We also used to have to dial the internet.)

It's easy to overlook details when they become routine. But in trading, the smallest errors can cause the biggest problems. That's why most companies have "buddy-check" systems in which two sets of eyes look at every payment, every hedge, and every contract. It may feel like overkill, but when millions are on the line, it's far better to be proactive than reactive.

13. Risk

Commodity trading is about balancing risk and reward. Every trade carries exposure - some risks can be identified, quantified, and mitigated before they become losses. Other risks can't be eliminated, but understanding how they arise and how they can be managed is central to protecting company profit and reputation.

We covered price risk and hedging in Chapter 11, but physical traders face many different types of risk daily. The best traders aren't those who avoid risk, but those who understand it better than their competitors.

Market Risk

Market risk is the exposure to the underlying market moving against your position. Companies that hedge their outright price exposures are still susceptible to losses from their physical positions.

Traders *can* create profits on "back-to-back" trades, matching physical purchases to sales, locking in a margin and taking minimal market risk. But physical markets rarely move in perfect symmetry. Often traders must take a position, either long or short physical, in expectation of future market moves.

If a trader is long physical, they are hoping that market conditions will tighten before they sell, allowing them to capture more favorable sales terms. If it is short, it is betting that supply increases or demand weakens, letting it cover at profitable levels.

There is an inherent timing risk here; if physical markets do not move how traders expect, positions can be hard to reverse quickly. If a trader is long during a period of low demand, they will need to finance material for longer than expected, or sell at a loss. Conversely, traders that are short in a tight market may have to pay over-the-odds to fulfill their obligations.

Traders can diversify against this risk by having a global footprint. By gaining exposure to multiple regions it increases options for sourcing and consumption.

Logistical Risk

Physically moving commodities from production to consumption introduces exposure that is rarely within a trader's control. Port congestion, pipeline disruptions, vessel breakdowns, labor strikes, or even unexpected weather can derail the best laid plans.

Even minor logistical inefficiencies can add up, quickly turning a profit into a loss. Building strong relationships across the logistics chain, from shipping lines to truckers, barge operators, and storage companies, allows traders to respond quickly when the unexpected happens.

Traders with reliable, monthly volumes of goods on a specific route may enter into freight agreements for a fixed period - these agreements are known as "take or pay." The trader will be charged for the freight even if they don't use it, but the transport provider guarantees them capacity.

Even when cargoes are moving, risks remain. Theft and accidental loss are common in this industry, and with individual containers worth millions, insurance becomes essential. While insurance doesn't prevent these risks, it can protect balance sheets from catastrophic events.

Counterparty Risk

Counterparty risk falls into two main categories: financial, where a company does not pay for delivered goods; or operational, where a company fails to supply or take delivery after a contract has been agreed.

Trading companies use rigorous KYC and credit procedures, assessing not only a company's financial health but also its reputation. However, even long-established firms can default in times of high volatility, so ongoing monitoring of counterparties is crucial. A credit line that was extended at the start of a relationship is not guaranteed in perpetuity. Contracts can be renegotiated if performance does not meet the required standard. Physical contracts are often drafted with protections such as a material adverse change (MAC) clause, allowing a trader to suspend or terminate commitments if the counterparty's financial condition materially worsens. These clauses help ensure traders are not contractually obligated to deliver to a company that may no longer be able to pay or perform.

Diversifying across customers, suppliers, and even commodities helps prevent concentration risk. Trade credit insurance is another tool that traders use, in which insurers provide reimbursement if a customer defaults. However, insurance should complement good risk assessment, not replace it.

Operational Risk

At the time of writing, physical trading remains heavily manual. Internal errors, missed hedges, delays in documentation, or even system failures are common causes of operational loss.

The commodities industry is fast-paced with high volume and razor-thin margins; even small mistakes can severely affect profitability.

This is why commodity firms spend heavily on systems, automation, and controls. Duties are segregated between front, middle, and back-office. Positions are reconciled daily, and training is an ongoing process. Senior staff who understand the cost of errors are relied on to impart that knowledge to other team members.

Financing and Liquidity Risk

Physical commodities are among the most capital-intensive businesses in the world. Changes in interest rates, collateral requirements, and credit lines can materially affect profitability.

Traders are typically long physical before they are short, so trading frequently requires holding inventory. But carry costs - storage, interest, and insurance - can often change, turning profitable trades into losses if not adequately accounted for.

The finance team's role is critical: building and maintaining strong banking relationships, diversifying funding sources, and monitoring the company's liquidity in real-time. Some traders also hedge borrowing costs using interest rate swaps to protect against rising rates.

While most traders hedge against outright price risk, hedging introduces another challenge - margin risk. Open futures positions marked-to-market daily. If the market moves against them, traders must post variation margin. Often traders are able to use credit lines to finance variation margin but once those lines are exhausted, margin calls require cash.

Failure to pay margin calls has catastrophic consequences for a trader's credit standing and ability to operate. To mitigate this risk, the finance team must work hand in hand with front and middle-office to sufficiently plan and stress-test positions against black swan events.

An example of such an event occurred in March 2022, when a crisis on the LME nickel contract saw prices more than triple within forty-eight hours. Several traders and brokers faced margin calls so large that they were pushed to the brink of insolvency. This event highlights just how fragile access to liquidity can be when volatility spikes.

Reputational Risk

As commodity trading has entered the public sphere, traders are expected to demonstrate transparency, sustainability, and ethical integrity.

Any perceived breach of ESG standards, environmental damage, or ethical violations can lead to the loss of bank lines, customers, or even trading licenses.

Many traders now employ internal or external public relations teams to manage communications proactively. But the best protection is a strong internal culture of due diligence, supplier audits, and immediate escalation of potential issues.

Force Majeure Risk

Occasionally an event will occur that is entirely unexpected and outside the control of a trader. Natural disasters, mine collapses, and oil leaks can all make performance of contracts impossible.

Force majeure clauses allow for a pause, or sometimes cancellation of a contract if such an event occurs. The specific circumstances that permit a force majeure declaration will be clearly defined in the physical contract.

In September of 2025, the Grasberg copper mine in Indonesia, the world's second largest copper mine, suffered a mudslide that sent 800,000 tons of wet material into the pit, killing seven workers and halting operations indefinitely. Force majeure was declared across supply contracts, leaving traders scrambling to replace tonnage elsewhere.

A similar dynamic played out in the energy markets in 2010 when a blowout occurred during well-completion operations on the Deepwater Horizon drilling rig operated by BP, approximately forty miles off the coast of Louisiana. The resulting explosion and fire caused the rig to sink, killing 11 workers and releasing an estimated 4.9 million barrels of crude into the Gulf of Mexico.

The incident became the largest accidental marine oil spill in history and prompted the United States government to impose a moratorium on deepwater drilling. As a result, force majeure was declared across numerous crude supply, transport, and oilfield service contracts due to regulatory shutdowns and the physical impossibility of continuing operations.

Deepwater Horizon established an important precedent: environmental disasters combined with government intervention can qualify as force majeure, even where the original trigger was operational failure rather than a natural event.

While such events cannot be predicted, they can be prepared for. Diversified sourcing, contingency plans, and clear contractual language are the best protection for a trader.

Political Risk

International trade depends on political stability and predictable policy. Changes to both can occur overnight. Export bans, sanctions, tariffs, and changes in taxation can all alter trade flows and profitability.

Staying close to regulatory developments and building language into contracts that protects against changes in law or sanctions can help traders mitigate this risk.

In some instances, such as the 2022 sanctions against Russian oil that sent energy markets into a tailspin, traders were able to make record profits as they captured arbitrage opportunities, repositioning cargoes to take advantage of the volatility.

Risk is inevitable in physical trading. But it is incumbent on every desk, from front to middle to back-office to identify, understand, and mitigate risks whenever possible.

A trader cannot eliminate all risk, because without it there would be no opportunity. The objective is to make informed decisions that balance potential reward against acceptable risk.

Chapter Summary

- Every trade carries risk. A trader's role is to identify, quantify, and mitigate risks before they become losses.
- Traders can hedge their outright price risk but still face the market risk of premiums or discounts moving against their positions. Diversification across regions and products helps reduce exposure.
- Logistical risk stems from delays, disruptions, or losses during transport. Using reliable partners, purchasing insurance, and contingency planning are crucial.
- Counterparty risk includes financial default or failure to perform. KYC procedures help mitigate exposure.
- Operational risk covers internal errors, system failures, and poor controls. Clearly defined duties, daily reconciliations, and strong training can reduce this risk.
- Financing and liquidity risk come from the high working capital required to trade commodities. Planning and close coordination between trading and finance teams is critical.
- Reputational risk arises from ESG violations, unethical conduct, or poor communication. Maintaining strong corporate governance and transparency protects a company's standing.
- Force majeure risk reflects unforeseeable events such as natural disasters or accidents. Clear contractual language and diversified sourcing can limit the impact.
- Political risk can include sanctions, export bans, tariffs, and taxation changes. Flexible contract structuring is key to reducing this risk.
- Effective risk management involves identifying the known risks, quantifying them, and mitigating exposure where possible, while retaining enough risk to capture profit.

Hidden Danger of LME Week

Those of you who have attended an LME week, or any large trading conference, are aware of the usual pitfalls. Too many drinks, late nights, and the inevitable cold you pick up from shaking far too many hands. But other dangers are lurking.

London, like any major city, is not immune to crime. And unfortunately, business travelers are often targeted. On this particular evening, AC and two of his companions had just finished dinner at one of Mayfair's fine restaurants. As they casually strolled down the street to catch a taxi, an assailant approached them from behind.

Quick as a flash he had latched on to the client's arm, clearly after his limited-edition timepiece. What the thief had not accounted for was just how much (Dutch) courage AC had developed over the course of the evening. Channeling as much inner Magnum P.I. energy as his newly grown mustache would allow, he launched himself at the attacker and dragged him to the ground.

While the scuffle continued, a second attacker approached, this one brandishing a brick from a nearby building site. He was clearly looking to avenge his fallen comrade.

"I'll see your brick and raise you two guns." shouted AC, flexing his arms in what police would later describe as a "Hulk-like pose". The attacker attempted to throw the brick at AC but to no avail as he was driven back by pure testosterone.

Moments later, London's finest were on the scene causing the attackers to flee, leaving a slightly exhausted AC to debrief the police.

Commodity trading forces you to keep your wits about you, and recognize risks that others might not see. In this instance, those instincts helped AC prevent a life-threatening situation and cemented his standing in his client's book.

14. Fundamental Analysis

A cornerstone of physical commodity trading is the analyzing market supply and demand. This is commonly known as the market fundamentals - how much of a given commodity is currently in supply, compared to the overall consumption. The result of this comparison is known as a market balance. If a market is oversupplied, it is said to be in a surplus. If the market is undersupplied, it is said to be in a deficit.

Fundamental analysis is performed on local, regional, and global levels. A market might be in a global surplus but certain regions could experience acute shortages due to supply constraints or logistics bottlenecks. Trading companies will position themselves accordingly to take advantage of any geographic dislocations in supply and demand, selling into regions of deficit and sourcing from regions of surplus.

Fundamental analysis differs from technical analysis, which focuses on price charts and patterns to attempt to predict future price movements. Fundamental analysis instead seeks to understand the underlying physical and economic forces that drive production, consumption, inventories, and trade flows.

Various drivers of supply need to be monitored constantly, and some are not always immediately clear. Larger, more public figures such as production capacity, mining output, and refinery utilization rates are usually easy to come by. However, secondary drivers such as scrap generation that is often spread over hundreds, if not thousands of suppliers, are much harder to consistently analyze.

The climate over the long-term and weather trends in the short to medium-term can have huge impacts on supply of agricultural commodities. When a single weather event can affect an entire season of copes, it is crucial to understand its impact on global supply. Some larger agricultural traders have in-house meteorologists or dedicated climate teams for this reason.

Government policy plays a major role in shaping global supply dynamics.

Control over a country's raw materials is often carefully managed by the government. Trade policy can change as frequently as administrations do, and its impacts can be instrumental on traders' market positions.

Two recent examples of how government policy affects supply dynamics occurred in the metals space. In January 2020 Indonesia, producer of 50 percent of the world's mined nickel, banned the export of nickel ores and concentrates, aiming to force domestic processing. The Democratic Republic of the Congo (DRC) is the world's largest producer of cobalt at ~75 percent of global supply. In February 2025 the DRC introduced a temporary export ban on cobalt to support the international price by controlling supply.

The same principle can be seen in the oil market. The Organization of the Petroleum Exporting Countries (OPEC), led by Saudi Arabia and Russia, has frequently adjusted production quotas to influence global crude oil prices. By coordinating output cuts or increasing supply, OPEC manages the global supply and demand balance.

Local elements of production such as power costs and labor availability can also influence supply. Increases in power prices can make production uneconomical, while strikes or political instability can create unexpected production gaps.

On the demand side, macroeconomic figures such as industrial production and GDP growth help determine consumption across a range of commodities by country. Increasing GDP tends to be correlated with increased demand for raw materials as consumer purchasing power increases. At the same time, declining GDP, rising unemployment rates, and other recessionary warning signs can signal lower future demand.

Commodity traders must maintain accurate understanding of consumer behavior and seasonal patterns that will influence demand. For example, seasonal stockpiling often occurs in China ahead of long public holidays such as the Lunar New Year and Golden Week. During these periods, many factories and ports slow down or temporarily shut, so buyers prefer to secure materials in advance to ensure uninterrupted production once operations resume. This behavior often leads to a temporary increase in import volumes and spot buying of copper, aluminum, iron ore, and crude oil in the preceding weeks. However, if these typical increases are not observed, it can also provide traders with insights into potential decreases in demand overall.

Government policy influences not only the supply of commodities but also domestic demand. Stimulus packages, infrastructure projects, tax incentives, and decreases in regulation are just some ways that governments can boost consumption. For countries such as China and the United States, these changes can have enormous implications for global demand.

Strategic reserves can also play a role in shaping commodity demand. China and the United States have long maintained stockpiles of commodities deemed critical to national security. More recently other countries including Australia, Japan, and the European Union have also begun developing a reserve of critical raw materials.

Technological change further reshapes commodity balances. As the adoption of electric vehicles accelerates, demand for battery metals such as nickel, lithium, and cobalt has surged, while demand for refined lead - used primarily in starter batteries for combustion-engine vehicles - is likely to decline. Similarly, as the world looks to reduce reliance on fossil fuels, we will continue to see shifts in demand for crude and refined products, along with increasing demand for replacement commodities.

Substitution effects also play a role in fundamental analysis. If one commodity is deemed too expensive, consumers may try to find alternatives. For example, at the time of writing copper is approximately four times more expensive than aluminum. But it requires approximately 1.6 times more aluminum to carry the same current as copper. There are other benefits of copper over aluminium for wiring such as tensile strength and flexibility, but as price differentials widen, consumers may be more inclined to switch to aluminum. Once production has been changed, it is often not quick or straightforward to revert, which can destroy demand forever.

An often-overlooked aspect of fundamental analysis is inventory levels. Inventories are a bridge between supply and demand. Global commodity stock data are published and can serve as a reference point for overall market balance. High or increasing inventory levels can indicate oversupply, whereas low or decreasing inventory levels can indicate market tightness. The rate of change in these inventories can often be a better indicator of changing global sentiment than the outright inventory level itself.

Public inventory levels are easy to capture and track. But commodities are often held in private storage "off exchange," making it difficult to put a precise number on the volume. Traders will leverage their vast logistics networks - ports, warehouses, and storage facilities - to try and incorporate any hidden or invisible inventory into their models to improve accuracy.

While the immediate impacts of changes in supply and demand are often reflected in a commodity's outright price, a company does not have to take speculative positions in the futures market to require an accurate supply and demand picture of the commodities it trades. The ability to adjust physical trading positions in response to changing market fundamentals drives profits for physical traders.

Traders will use their knowledge of supply and demand to inform their physical trading decisions. Whether that is to be long or short a physical commodity, or build long-term plans based on the expected future supply and demand picture.

While numerous commodity research firms frequently publish supply and demand balances, traders often combine these figures with their own in-house analysis based on physical contracts with producers and consumers. This approach can usually give them a more accurate and closely monitored picture. If a trader has large supply agreements with major consumers, they will likely be the first one to know if demand is slowing because of lower order books or weaker margins.
Similarly, if a trader has significant offtake agreements with producers, it will have an insight into future production levels that other companies may

not.

Fundamental balances are not static. Seasonality, government policy, and technological shifts all influence supply and demand. In 2025 we saw the dramatic impact that tariffs had on historical trade flows, affecting regional balances almost overnight. Traders who reacted quickly and adapted their trading habits captured significant profits from those changes in regional supply.

While no system is perfect, accurately monitoring the shifts in fundamentals is a core component of physical commodity trading. It enables traders to identify arbitrage opportunities, optimize logistics, and align trading strategies with the real economy. A trader's profits often hinge on how they have positioned themselves based on these fundamentals.

Chapter Summary

- Market fundamentals form the foundation of physical trading, comparing supply to demand to ascertain if a market is in surplus or deficit.
- This analysis is performed on a local, regional, and global level to identify and capture dislocations and trading opportunities.
- Drivers of supply include production capacity, mining output, refinery utilization, scrap generation, energy costs, weather, labor, and government policy.
- Demand drivers include GDP growth, industrial production, consumer trends, seasonality, substitution, and technological change.
- Government policy such as export bans, tariffs, and stimulus programs also affects trade flows and regional demand.
- Inventory levels act as a bridge between supply and demand. The rate of change in these inventories is often more revealing than the inventory level itself.
- Public data are key but private and off-exchange inventories are crucial to determine accurate availability.
- Strong relationships with producers and consumers provide traders with real-time intelligence, often ahead of published data.
- Substitution effects can permanently shift demand patterns once production adjusts.
- Fundamentals are constantly evolving and traders who monitor and adapt quickly to shifts in trade flows gain a competitive advantage.

Lost in Translation

When I first moved from the United Kingdom to Switzerland, I expected a language barrier. English to German is hardly straightforward, and the occasional misunderstanding was inevitable.

But when I later moved to the United States, I assumed those days were behind me. Same language, right? How wrong I was.

Growing up in South East London, my accent isn't what anyone would describe as *the Queen's English.* The night I met my wife, she texted her mum saying, *"I've met someone who sounds like Russell Brand."* Fortunately, that's where the similarities between him and me end.

In my accent, Ts have a habit of disappearing, think *wa'er, ci'y, compu'er.* In contrast, Americans turn their Ts into Ds: *wader, cidy, compuder.* It's a subtle difference, but one that can change the course of a conversation entirely.

One Tuesday, I arrived early for lunch and sat at the bar to wait for my client. When the bartender asked what I wanted, I casually said, "A large glass of wa'er, please." She gave me a brief, puzzled look, then poured me a generous measure of neat vodka.

Either I looked like someone who drank heavily before noon, or she figured anyone in commodities could use the distraction. I quickly clarified and received what I'd actually asked for - a large glass of *wa**d**er.*

It was a harmless mix-up, but it stuck with me. In trading, miscommunications can cost far more than a mistaken drink order. We had a guy on the desk with a thick French accent. He placed a spread trade "for a hundred lots," which the broker heard as "four hundred lots." The desk head almost had a heart attack when he saw the fill come through.

Exchange brokers often juggle multiple orders at once. If your instructions aren't obvious, they may not stop to clarify; they'll just execute. It's always worth clarifying when placing an order and immediately after executing to ensure there were no misunderstandings.

15. Global Influences on Commodities

In the last chapter we discussed the importance of monitoring commodity supply and demand. But what actually influences these flows at the micro and macro levels? What are the forces that cause production or consumption to shift, sometimes gradually, sometimes overnight?

Countless variables can affect commodity production and consumption, but a few key standouts are worth noting when considering this industry. Understanding them allows traders to anticipate changes before they are reflected in official statistics.

US Dollar

Outside of a few regional exchanges, commodities are by and large priced in US dollars (USD). However, the global nature of commodity trading involves physical transactions in every global currency. If a commodity company is transacting in a currency other than USD, it will need to convert the local currency to USD in order to complete the transaction. The prevailing foreign exchange rate will have a material impact on the commodity's cost.

For example, a European buyer of refined zinc that is pricing its purchase on the LME, which settles in USD. If the LME price of zinc is $3,000/mt and the EUR/USD exchange rate is 1.16, then in Euro terms, the buyer is paying €2,586/mt. However, if the EUR/USD rate appreciates to 1.18, then the purchase becomes relatively cheaper in Euros, now costing €2,542/mt, despite the price on the LME remaining $3,000/mt.

In contrast, if the EUR depreciates and the rate changes to 1.14, that same purchase with an LME price of $3,000/mt is now more expensive in Euros, costing €2,632/mt.

Changes in the relative strength of the USD to other global currencies can have a material impact on the global demand for commodities. While it is not a perfect correlation, a stronger dollar makes commodities more expensive in local currency terms, which can dampen demand. Because of this, a strong dollar is linked to lower commodity prices - higher costs lead to decreased demand, which can push USD priced commodities lower to compensate.

Conversely, a weaker USD can boost demand as commodities become relatively cheaper in local currency terms. Lower global costs can increase demand and raise commodity prices in USD.

This is a very high-level and simplistic view but it is important to understand the historical context and why commodity markets pay such close attention to things such as US Federal Reserve (Fed) interest rate decisions. When the Fed enters a cycle of interest rate cuts, the argument goes that the USD should continue to weaken. As interest rates are lowered, the yield on US bonds decreases, making them less attractive to foreign investors. This in turn decreases demand for USD, and the dollar weakens.

In contrast, if the Fed is in a cycle of interest rate rises, perhaps in an attempt to cap inflation, there will be upward pressure on the USD as the yield on US bonds increases, making them more attractive to foreign investors, increasing demand for USD.

However, because global demand is such a complex and interconnected picture, a weakening USD does not guarantee higher commodity prices (or vice versa with a strengthening dollar). If the market believes that the Fed is being forced into large rate cuts because the United States is headed for recession (along with other global economies), that may have an offsetting or even larger negative impact on global demand for commodities. Hence, we may see reduced prices in the near term - though like most reactions to news announcements, the initial responses are usually knee-jerk rather than well-thought-out long-term decisions.

Other major economies also have their own central banks that set interest rates. Analyzing global rate differentials - not just US moves in isolation - is key to understanding the broader macro environment for commodities.

Increased interest rates also raise financing costs for traders and producers, making it more expensive to hold inventory or fund production. Conversely, when interest rates fall, commodity-intensive sectors such as construction and manufacturing typically expand, boosting consumption.

Geopolitics

In the 20th and 21st century as globalization made the world more interconnected, barriers were brought down from an international trading perspective. New trade routes were established and new corridors were created, aiding the flow of commodities. But this same interconnection has made commodities vulnerable to political disruption.

Governments change frequently, and each transition can bring policy changes. New trade agreements can be established, or tariffs and sanctions can be imposed. Every time a new policy is enacted, it can alter the global flow of commodities.

In 2022, the invasion of Ukraine by Russia brought huge sanctions against Russian energy production. This dramatically affected energy flows throughout the world. Europe, which had previously relied heavily on Russia for its energy supply, was forced to diversify its energy sources rapidly. Countries such as India and China sought to buy Russia's excess capacity at discounts as Russia now had limited options to sell.

In 2025 when the Trump administration imposed wide-ranging tariffs on most global economies, traders scrambled to adjust, mitigating exposures and attempting to profit from the supply disruptions the tariffs were creating.

It is not just international trade policy that has dramatic impacts on commodities - domestic policy can also significantly move markets. Governments are often heavily involved in infrastructure investments that require vast amounts of commodities in their development. From roads and bridges to energy grids and pipelines - all of these projects lead to increased demand for commodities.

China has been a significant example of government-backed infrastructure spending that has increased global supply and demand across the board. Stimulus announcements by the Chinese government frequently affect commodity markets, both positively, and negatively when spending is lower than expected.

Government regulation also affects commodity flow. To break ground on new commodity supply projects, companies typically need to obtain permission from local governments. In countries with lower regulation and government oversight, permits can be easily obtained. However, in locations with tightening environmental or safety oversight, project lead times and costs can rise sharply, reducing potential new supply.

As regulatory oversight changes, the expected supply of a commodity can change. And because of the long-term nature of supply projects - sometimes taking years from permitting and actual production - trading companies need to pay keen attention to these changes to form short and long-term views.

Climate

In 2015, 195 countries signed and ratified the Paris agreement - committing to keeping global warming below 2°C, ideally 1.5°C above preindustrial levels. If the world is to achieve these ambitions, it will take a dramatic shift in both human behavior and historical demand for certain commodities.

As the global economy shifts toward renewable energy and decarbonization, demand for certain raw materials has increased sharply. Metals such as copper, aluminum, nickel, lithium, cobalt, and rare earth elements are essential for building the infrastructure needed for electrification - from power grids and batteries to wind turbines and electric vehicles.

Most of the Western world is now playing catch-up as greater volumes of these raw materials are produced outside those countries. Vast quantities of the world's critical materials are mined in countries that are not direct allies, creating an environment rife with dramatic price swings outside of the sphere of US and EU influence. For example, China dominates rare earth refining, the DRC accounts for the majority of cobalt supply, and Indonesia and the Philippines are the leading producers of nickel.

Adding to this complexity, ESG regulations in Western economies have made it increasingly difficult to access these critical minerals. The paradox is that the push for sustainability has, in some cases, made it harder to source the very materials required for the transition.

For traders, the intersection of climate policy and resource geography is now one of the defining forces shaping long-term commodity flows and pricing.

Logistics and Infrastructure

Even when supply and demand appear balanced, disruptions to logistics can distort that reality. The ability, or inability, to efficiently move material through the global supply chain can determine whether a market feels long or short in practice.

Transportation, storage, and infrastructure such as ports and pipelines are the backbone of the commodities world. Any disruption to this system can dramatically alter trade flows and prices. A region may have a surplus of material. Still, if there is port congestion or a lack of freight, that material can become trapped, creating local oversupply and shortages in consumption locations.

For example, during the early stages of the European energy crisis after Russia invaded Ukraine in 2022, Europe struggled to import enough LNG to replace Russian pipeline gas. While the United States had abundant LNG available for export, Europe lacked sufficient regasification terminals to handle volumes arriving by vessel.

During the COVID-19 pandemic, some metals and raw materials became stranded at origin as container freight rates spiked. The lack of port workers caused vessels to face lengthy unloading times, often sitting in port for weeks. Even though production had not fallen, the vessel bottleneck caused supply to fall and prices to spike.

Infrastructure investment is another long-term influence on commodities. The construction of new pipelines, rail links, or port expansions can open entirely new trade routes. China's Belt and Road Initiative for example, a global infrastructure and economic development strategy launched in 2013, has reshaped supply chains across Asia and Africa, increasing connectivity between inland mines and coastal ports. Similarly, the expansion of the Panama Canal in 2016 altered the economics of trans-Atlantic and trans-Pacific shipping, especially for bulk cargoes such as coal, LNG, and grains.

A trader who has the correct view on supply and demand but lacks the logistical capability to implement that strategy can fail in execution.

Technology and Innovation

Technological advancement has always shaped commodity markets, but the pace of change in the early twenty-first century has been extraordinary. From the rapid rise of artificial intelligence (AI), to breakthroughs in battery chemistry, technology is now one of the defining forces influencing both short and long-term demand for commodities.

The explosive growth of AI has driven unprecedented investment in energy-intensive data centers, advanced semiconductors, and high-performance computing hardware. For every gigawatt of energy AI uses, an additional 30,000mt of refined copper for electrical cabling is required. Vast quantities of aluminum are needed for cooling and structural components. The power consumption of these data centers has increased demand across electricity, natural gas, and renewable energy markets. There has been a global race to secure chip manufacturing - increasing demand for specialty metals such as gallium, germanium, and tungsten.

At the same time, technological change is reshaping the composition of demand within commodities. The transition to electric vehicles (EVs) for example has dramatically altered the mix of required materials. Initial EV technology was heavily dependent on cobalt and nickel, but new technologies such as lithium-iron-phosphate (LFP) have reduced reliance on those metals, while increasing demand for lithium, graphite, and phosphate. As technology continues to evolve, there will be winners and losers among commodity producers.

Technology innovation also affects the supply of commodities. Automation and advanced process control are improving mine efficiency, reducing costs, and extending asset life. Improvements in metal recycling technologies are closing material loops that previously relied entirely on primary production.

While innovations can create massive demand, they can also cause demand destruction when substitution becomes available. The shift from internal combustion engines to EVs, or from coal-fired power to renewable energy is a prime example of technology eroding demand for one commodity while fueling growth in others.

Traders who understand emerging technologies and how they alter the underlying material mix will be far better equipped to anticipate where future tightness or oversupply will arise.

<u>Investment Flows and Speculation</u>

The prices of commodities are not solely driven by the physical supply and demand. They are also heavily influenced by financial flows. Investment funds and commodity trade advisors (CTAs) play a major role in price discovery.

When speculative traders build positions, markets can frequently overlook fundamentals in the short-term. Conversely, when speculators liquidate positions it can lead to violent corrections. Sometimes commodity prices can seem detached from the physical reality, and traders must interpret these market moves. The outright price of a commodity can impact future investment decisions, so even traders who hedge outright price risk must pay close attention to the speculative nature of commodity pricing.

Energy Costs

It is not just energy traders who follow energy prices and availability. Energy costs can dictate the viability of production for everything from aluminum smelting to fertilizer manufacturing. When oil and natural gas prices rise, commodity producers with energy-intensive operations see their margins compressed. The volatility of energy prices is directly correlated with commodity supply and can often lead to supply curtailments.

Between 2021 and 2022, Europe lost approximately 50 percent of its refined aluminum and zinc production because of soaring energy costs. At the same time, cheap gas in the United States has supported the domestic petrochemical and fertilizer businesses. The shale gas boom in the United States significantly lowered input costs, making production significantly cheaper than that in Europe and Asia.

As global decarbonization efforts expand, energy availability and cost will increasingly determine where energy-intensive industries locate, influencing the long-term geography of production.

Weather and Natural Disasters

While there is an obvious link between the weather and the agricultural industry, it can affect nearly every commodity. Droughts can affect water levels, constraining barge and vessel availability for moving metals and grains. Hurricanes in the Gulf frequently disrupt crude oil and LNG exports. While natural disasters can initially decrease demand in that region, rebuilding efforts afterwards often require significant volumes of commodities. Increasing global temperatures can energy grids as demand for air conditioning rises.

Weather introduces short and long-term volatility that even the most sophisticated models struggle to predict. Traders who understand seasonal risk are much better prepared to manage exposures that others often overlook.

Labor and Social Stability

Beyond physical disruptions, the stability of supply also depends on the availability and skills of the people and communities behind production. Labor disputes, strikes, or social unrest frequently disrupt mines, smelters, and infrastructure such as ports and rail operations.

A recurring example is Chile, the world's largest copper producer. Chile accounts for roughly 25 percent of the global mined copper supply, so even minor disruptions can impact global supply chains. Labor negotiations between unions and mining companies are often tense, particularly during periods of high metal prices when workers seek a greater share of profits.

In 2021, workers at Escondida, the world's largest copper mine, threatened a prolonged strike over pay and benefits. A similar walkout in 2017 had already paralyzed production for forty-four days, removing nearly 120,000 mt of copper from the market - equivalent to 2 percent of global monthly supply at the time. The mere threat of another strike in 2021 was enough to lift copper prices as traders priced in potential shortages.

Another example is the DRC, which produces over 70 percent of the world's cobalt and a growing share of copper. The DRC's mining sector has been repeatedly disrupted by regional conflict, protests over working conditions, accusations of child labor, and disputes with local communities over mining concessions. In 2019, tensions at the Mutanda mine - then the world's largest cobalt producer - escalated, leading to clashes and temporary shutdowns. Production at the mine was later suspended for economic and operational reasons, removing an estimated 20 percent of global cobalt supply from the market.

These examples underline how fragile the supply side of commodities can be when social tensions rise. Labor relations and community stability can take years to build, and only moments to break down. Traders who track the social and political climate in commodity-producing nations often gain early insight into potential supply disruptions long before they make headline news.

Successful traders view all these influences not as isolated variables, but as an interconnected system in which monetary policy, logistics, and human behavior combine to shape the real-world movement and pricing of commodities.

Chapter Summary

- Multiple forces beyond simple supply and demand shape commodity flows.
- The US dollar and interest rate cycles significantly impact purchasing power, financing costs, and speculative positioning across all commodities.
- Geopolitical and domestic policy shifts, from sanctions and tariffs to infrastructure investment, can instantly reroute global trade flows and alter demand.
- Climate policy and the energy transition have redefined material demand, driving new dependencies on critical minerals while ESG regulations tighten supply in Western economies.
- Logistics and infrastructure determine whether supply can reach demand.
- Advancements in technology reshape what materials are consumed, and how they are produced.
- Speculative trading can move prices away from fundamentals, creating both risk and opportunity for physical traders.
- Energy costs and availability dictate production viability across the commodity complex, often triggering curtailments or regional advantages.
- Weather and natural disasters inject volatility into both production and consumption.
- Labor unrest and social instability can remove supply overnight in key producing regions.

Arrested Cargo

Sometimes, if a deal sounds too good to be true, and in commodity trading, if something feels off, it usually is.

We were looking at buying a cargo of refined lead from Puerto Rico, not the most obvious origin but the discounts being offered made it worth investigating.

I couldn't make the trip myself so the head of the office and someone from the credit team flew out to inspect the facility. Everything seemed above board - clean operation, decent financials, and no reason to raise immediate alarm bells.

However, when the contract arrived one clause stood out. Payment would not be made against a standard BOL, but against confirmation from the shipping line that cargo had been loaded.

I was uneasy about this, as was the credit department, but when we raised the issue the head of the office brushed it aside "If something goes wrong, I'll pay for it myself."

So, we make payment as agreed and await the BOL so we can collect the material at discharge. Two days went by with radio silence. Another two days, still nothing. We send the proof-of-loading document to the shipping line and that's when things start to unravel.

"I'm afraid that signature does not belong to anyone at the shipping line."

I ran over to my operator, "T, who did the email come from with the loading confirmation, the shipping line or the supplier?"

"The supplier, why?"

We had a serious problem. We had paid against a fraudulent confirmation and had no idea how many other companies may have done the same.

With few options left we contacted the port authorities. After reviewing the proof of payment and the forged documents, it was agreed that a U.S. Marshall would meet the vessel and impound the cargo until ownership could be verified.

It turns out that the supplier was facing some serious personal debt and had been running a small-scale Ponzi scheme, selling the same parcels of lead to multiple buyers, using new payments to plug previous holes and keep production afloat.

On a more extended voyage, this would have been easier for the supplier to navigate but on a short trip with both companies claiming the metal at discharge, the Ponzi scheme collapsed.

Luckily for us, our payment for the goods had been first so legally we were the rightful owners. But it could just as easily have been the other way around.

Let's just say that my boss was sweating when I asked him if he was getting his checkbook to reimburse the loss before we finally took delivery.

Gut instinct is a powerful tool in commodity trading. This often comes with experience but even early on in your career, if something doesn't feel right, trust your intuition. It is far better to be safe than sorry.

16. Decision-Making in Physical Trading

Commodity trading is often viewed in terms of numbers, but at its core it is a people-driven business. Front, middle, and back-office must make daily decisions amid uncertainty - when data may be incomplete, time is limited, and variables outside their control often influence outcomes.

Unlike speculative trading, physical trading decisions cannot be undone with a click. Every action, whether that is booking a vessel, agreeing on incoterms, or fixing a price, carries operational and financial consequences that sometimes unfold over months. This chapter will explore the mindset and frameworks that underpin effective decision-making in the physical commodity world.

Information Asymmetry

No trader ever has a perfect view of the market. Prices, stock levels, supply and demand, and freight availability are constantly shifting. The best traders know how to act decisively in an imperfect picture. They use their experience, relationships, and timing to narrow the uncertainty and position themselves to capitalize on potential dislocations.

For example, a trader hears from a consumer that stock levels are low in a specific region. If they act on this information before it becomes common knowledge, they will be best positioned to capture the arbitrage. However, if the story does not play out, there is a risk of loss through double-handling material.

Knowing how to distinguish between signals and noise - when to trust your information and when to wait for confirmation - is a key part of physical trading.

Balancing Risk with Reality

Every physical trade is a mix of opportunity and risk. Fixing a long-term freight contract may reduce costs, but it commits the trader to filling the vessels. Accumulating inventory in a high-contango environment may position a trader correctly for an expected supply deficit, but it ties up financing lines and capital that could be utilized elsewhere.

Selling to a customer with weaker credit may command a higher price and potential profit but carries a higher risk of default. Similarly, buying a specific production that is not exchange-registered may reduce sourcing costs, but reduces consumption points should the physical market dry up.

Physical commodity decision-making involves weighing financial upside against logistical, credit, and financing risks, not just market exposure. The ability to balance opportunities for profit with disciplined risk management is often what separates consistently successful traders from the rest.

Negotiation Psychology

Building strong relationships with counterparts is paramount in physical trading. Effective negotiation requires a balance - aggressive tactics may win some deals but can jeopardize future opportunities. Decision-making often hinges on trust, timing, and tone of a conversation.

For example, extending credit to a reputable customer facing short-term cash flow uncertainty may preserve a strategic relationship that returns years of repeat business. Or agreeing to a higher-than-market premium with a producer in exchange for securing a multi-year offtake agreement.

Negotiation in commodities is rarely zero-sum; the goal is more often mutual benefit. Understanding counterparty motivations is what turns transactional interactions into long-lasting partnerships.

Managing Time

Commodity traders operate in an environment where time is both an asset and a liability. Markets move quickly, vessels get delayed, and financing windows open and close. The ability to stay composed under pressure, prioritize tasks, and delegate effectively so that panic decisions are avoided often separates profitable desks from losing ones.

Human instinct often drives impulsive reactions to change, but experienced traders pause long enough to quantify exposure, review positions, and communicate options before making a decision.

Effective decision-making under time pressure isn't all about speed; it is about clarity and control.

Cognitive Biases

Even the most experienced traders can fall victim to subtle psychological traps:

- Anchoring bias: Relying too heavily on past conditions can prevent adapting to evolving markets. A trader convinced that a price or premium will return to prior levels may wait too long to make a decision.
- Confirmation bias: Part of trading is forming a view on the markets, but in doing so, traders must avoid only seeking information that supports their view. Traders need to be able to dissect multiple sources of information to give one balanced, coherent picture that informs their strategy.
- Sunk cost fallacy: Continuing to hold a position because of the cost or effort already invested can lead to large losses. Traders must recognize when to cut losses regardless of the amount invested.

Markets do not owe traders anything, and the ability to recognize and mitigate these biases allows traders to make rational decisions even when market volatility spikes. As the famous John Maynard Keynes quote goes, "The market can remain irrational longer than you can remain solvent."

Learning from Mistakes

In physical trading, errors are inevitable - whether from poorly timed commercial decisions or operational failures. What separates great traders from bad ones is not the absence of mistakes, but how they respond to them.

Establishing a process for documenting errors, mitigating their impact, and sharing lessons across teams fosters an environment where mistakes are less likely to recur.

Companies that embrace procedural improvements, develop best practices, and create positive feedback loops reduce the risk of systemic errors.

Decision-making in physical trading requires combining analysis with intuition and gut feeling. Successful traders need to be precise yet flexible, combining ambition with risk awareness. Seeking the best result in an uncertain environment requires a creative, adaptive, and disciplined mindset.

Chapter Summary

- Commodity trading decisions are made amid uncertainty. Success depends on judgment, timing, and adaptability, not perfect information.
- Great traders can balance financial opportunity with operational, logistical, and credit realities.
- Effective negotiation relies on trust and mutual benefit. Focusing on price alone is the wrong approach.
- Staying calm under pressure and recognizing cognitive biases allows traders to make rational, disciplined decisions in volatile environments.
- The best traders learn from mistakes and institutionalize those lessons, leading to better decision-making over time.

Time To Kill

C is a bit of a gun fanatic. Being British, I am still not used to that part of US culture. Still, C is at least a genuinely responsible gun owner and takes gun safety to the extreme.

So when we found ourselves with a couple of hours to spare before meeting a client in Houston, Texas (where else?), C suggested I try a shooting range for the first time. C is a decent trader, but he's an excellent shooter, so I figured if anyone was going to bring me up to speed it was him.

We entered the range and approached the counter, "We'll take the Glock 19." C said with a slight grin.

I grabbed my ear protectors and safety goggles as C ran through the safety brief. Usually I ignored his ramblings about weapons, but this time I listened intently.

Having passed the listening test, it was time to put things into action. I was about to have my very own James Bond moment. Watch out, bad guys, you don't stand a chance.

I loaded the gun, disengaged the safety, and aimed. After emptying the twelve-round clip, I re-engaged the safety, released the magazine, locked the slide back, made sure there was no bullet in the chamber, and put the gun down, ready to see just how many headshots I'd got.

Except there were no headshots. There were no holes in the paper target at all, not one. I didn't understand. Meanwhile, C was struggling to hold back his laughter, "Not quite as easy as in the movies, huh?"

I spent the next hour learning about sight alignment, breathing, and recoil. By the end, I was fairly confident from about five yards. So burglars take note, just stand 10 yards away from me and you'll probably be fine.

As we were leaving I noticed my wrists were dusted with gunpowder. The range attendant handed me a receipt and said, “You’ll need this at the airport when the sniffer dogs come up to you.”

“We’ll also need it to expense the ammo.” C added.

Confidence in trading is important but so is understanding where you need to improve. Whether that’s on the firing range or behind the negotiating table…though hopefully you won’t need to use a weapon during a negotiation.

17. The Future: Digitization and Technology in Commodities

Relationships will always be a pillar of physical trading, and because of that, the industry is somewhat insulated from AI in the "it's coming for your job" sense. This will always be a people-first business - trust is required to build relationships and execute physical business. To build that trust, you need to spend time face-to-face with your customers and clients; that is something AI cannot replace.

However, it would be naive to think there are no parts of the commodity trading supply chain that could be improved through the integration of AI and new technologies, which are advancing rapidly.

Physical commodity trading is inherently archaic. Much of the commodity world still runs on PDFs, emails, and spreadsheets. Physical documents like BOLs are still the backbone of the industry, not to mention the manual data entry, credit checks, and other procedures that are currently required. All of these create significant overhead and constant risk of human error, which can lead to catastrophic losses.

This is where AI can play an important role in commodity trading. Not replacing relationships, but in improving efficiency within commodity companies, freeing up employee time to focus on profit-driving solutions rather than paperwork.

BOLs and Title Documents

As referenced above, the title for physical commodities still involves physically couriering BOLs or other title documents around the world. This creates exposure to theft, duplication, and loss. Companies are under constant threat of fraud, and the manual element in the transfer of title increases the likelihood of fraud.

By utilizing secure blockchain technology, these documents could be produced, tracked, and released only to the correct counterparties in a fraction of the time it currently takes. Delays at ports due to an unknown location of the original BOL would disappear. Financing material and processing payments could be completed in a much more efficient and secure manner.

The Digital Container Shipping Association (DCSA) and ICC are already piloting e-BOL standards.

Banks are, at the time of writing, testing blockchain-backed trade documentation with platforms built on the Ethereum-based framework, Quorum. Digitizing the process improves data quality, accelerates settlement times, and strengthens security for participants. They are also streamlining the financial aspects of commodity trade, such as issuing digital letters of credit and verifying documents.

All these improvements reduce the risk of demurrage, leading to faster release of cargoes. In an environment where a misplaced original BOL can hold up a vessel carrying millions of dollars' worth of goods, a digital title becomes a necessity.

AI in the Physical Supply Chain

From data entry to document processing, AI has practical applications that would create efficiencies across the middle and back-office. Manual data entry is highly prone to human error, and while details can be double-checked to ensure accuracy, this all takes time and increases costs.

At the time of writing there are already AI systems that can analyze business confirmation emails and create company-specific contracts. These systems can be integrated with existing contract management and risk management systems to establish precise hedging requirements.

Image recognition software can be used to verify materials against specifications, spotting inconsistencies in certificates of analysis far more quickly and accurately than the human eye.

AI can also be used for operational forecasting, predicting laytime delays or freight bottlenecks using weather and real-time port data. It can calculate the most efficient freight routes or transport modes where multiple options are available.

It can be used by credit desks to analyze counterparty risk, using pattern recognition to detect anomalies in payment behavior or trade flows. For example, an AI model trained on five years of shipment data could flag counterparties that consistently delay document submission, or change shipment dates, allowing the front office to intervene before risk escalates.

AI can analyze company positions in real time, suggesting optimal inventory allocations and trading strategies to maximize overall payoff. It could also create bespoke supply-and-demand models to assist traders with their strategies.

Data Integration and CTRM Evolution

Most commodity companies still operate multiple, often disconnected systems for trading, logistics, finance, and risk. The next step in digitization is integration, creating a single, unified data environment that connects the entire organization. AI tools can connect these systems in real time, ensuring every department is working from the same data. For the traders, this means faster insight into exposures and positions, without the need for manual reconciliation.

Translation Services

English is the common language of commodity trading, but traders often need to be able to converse with counterparties in local languages. AI translations have come a long way from the inaccurate responses you would get from an internet translation. Whether it is a simple conversation or the construction of a complex deal, AI can generate text or translate from any global language, removing what was once a considerable barrier.

ESG and Traceability

Commodities often change hands multiple times from production to delivery to end consumers. Banks increasingly require traceable chain-of-custody data to confirm that goods meet all ESG standards through the point of production. These data could be easily stored on the blockchain and identifiable to each batch of material produced from mine site to port.

Over time, traceability may become as important to the commercial terms of a contract as the purity or grade of a commodity. A commodity verified as ethically sourced could determine access to financing, or a production process certified with a low-carbon footprint may command a premium from consumers seeking to meet Scope three targets. As global reporting standards tighten, commodities without a traceable origin may eventually become impossible to finance.

Cybersecurity and Data Risk

As the industry digitizes, an inevitable vulnerability will emerge. Cyberattacks on ports, systems, or physical infrastructure can paralyze operations. Protecting data integrity and ensuring redundancy is now as critical as physical security at a storage location. Companies will need to ensure as systems become more connected, they become harder to break.

Technology will continue to accelerate, but the fundamental drivers of commodity trading - trust, timing, and judgment will remain unchanged. Automation will not replace people; it will change what employees do. The most valuable employees are those who can bridge commercial experience with digital literacy, understanding the intricacies of physical trading and how data flows through a system.

Chapter Summary

- While relationships and trust will always be the foundation of physical trading, technology is rapidly reshaping how businesses operate.
- Blockchain and digital title systems will replace couriered documents and reduce fraud risk and delays while streamlining financing and cargo release.
- AI integration across the supply chain - from document automation to credit risk and freight optimization - will allow employees to focus on higher-value decision making.
- CTRM and data integration will create visibility across trading units, improving speed and accuracy in decision-making.
- AI-driven translation and collaboration tools will further remove language and regional barriers, supporting seamless global communication.
- ESG traceability is becoming a differentiating factor, with verified low-carbon or ethically sourced materials commanding premiums and enabling financing.
- Cybersecurity and data resilience are now critical components of operational risk management.
- The traders and companies that excel will be those that bridge commercial experience with digital literacy.

Preheating is Not Just for Your Oven

There is something almost hypnotic about watching molten metal - the heat, the energy, the glow. It all pulls you in.

A few years ago I was visiting an aluminum smelter with some of my colleagues. I always tried to take the middle office with me on customer visits so they could broaden their on-the-ground experience. I didn't expect this trip to end with them double-checking their life insurance.

We were being shown how recycled aluminum was melted down in a reverb furnace. The facility manager (who looked like he'd been forged in the same furnace he was currently working on) was explaining how they charged the furnace - alternating layers of molten bath and solid ingots.

Everything looked routine, the temperature read over 700°C, and we were about to see the next ingots go in. One of the junior furnace operators pushed the blocks in. Clean, bright, and harmless, or so he thought. But unbeknownst to him, the ingots had spent the night outside where a sudden downpour had left them soaked. Though they looked dry, small pockets of water were trapped within the porous surface.

The ingots hit the molten pool with a dull thud, and for a couple of seconds, nothing happened. Then the world went white. A deafening blast tore through the furnace as superheated steam burst out of the blocks. The pressure shot molten aluminum out like a cannon. Silver droplets sprayed through the air, hissing as they hit the concrete floors and walls.

We all ducked instinctively. Thankfully we were far enough back that no one was hurt. The manager shook his head and said to us, "Preheat everything; moisture and molten metal don't mix".

As we watched the automatic safety procedures kick in and awaited the fire department's arrival we all shared the same thoughts. All of this was caused by a few drops of water and a failure to follow procedures.

It can seem tempting to skip small steps in the interest of time, or convenience, but if you do, you risk blowing up a trade, in this case, literally.

18. How I Broke Into Commodities and Breaking into Commodity Trading Today

I graduated with a degree in economics in 2008, just before the Great Recession. Like most other graduates, I had been told I would walk into my dream job but this turned out not to be the case. I could have returned to a full-time position in accounts at RBS where I completed a summer internship, but the only thing I knew for sure was that I did not want to stare at a spreadsheet for nine hours a day as a career.

Nine months went by of trying to cobble enough work together so my dad did not have to pay his twenty-one-year-old son 10 pounds again to wash his car. I was actually a pretty good football referee when I was younger and could have gone down that route, but I do not enjoy thousands of people swearing at me in chorus. So, I stuck to my goal of doing something in the financial markets; I just did not know what.

Then pretty much out of the blue, I got a call from my recruiter telling me about an operator job at Trafigura. I knew nothing about them or commodities, but I headed to my brother's office where he showed me everything that had happened with oil prices in the prior six months.

I walked into the interview brimming with unearned confidence and ready to show off my oil trading acumen, only to be greeted by the COO of metals and the global head of copper concentrates trading. It turned out the potential role was on the refined metals desk.

The first question they asked me was "What do you know about physical metals trading?" Expecting this to be an oil role I was completely unprepared. I had to make a split-second decision - do I try and BS my way through this answer, or should I be honest? I opted for the latter, which is always the correct decision. "I know the difference between physical and paper trading but that's about it. But I guarantee you, if you give me this opportunity I will soak up information like a sponge and be able to have a tangible positive impact on the desk".

I am not sure if they could sense any of the desperation I was trying to hide, but they seemed to appreciate the answer. We spent much of the rest of the interview discussing that we grew up in neighboring towns - the importance of active listening in interviews and turning them into conversations cannot be overstated.

A few days later I flew out to Lucerne, Switzerland, for a trial day where I booked some trucks, checked stock positions, and chatted with people on the desk. The work I did that day was not important; the real test was how I interacted with people - would they want to work with me for nine hours a day?

Thankfully, the global head of operations offered me the role and, after eating some chocolates while looking out at the Alps over Lake Lucerne, I gladly accepted. I would never get over those views as I walked to work each morning - not that the views in South East London aren't as scenic of course.

My trial day happened to be St. Patrick's Day and I was told to head over to the local Irish pub, Mr. Pickwick, to celebrate with some of the other expats and my future colleagues. After having a great night and indulging in perhaps a few too many drinks, I went back to the hotel and drifted off happily.

Waking up the following morning, I stared at my phone through bleary eyes and panic shot through me. I slept through the five alarms I set and missed my flight. Side note - if you are going into this industry you should get used to being put on the first possible flight out in the morning.

I headed to Zurich airport, after stopping for a lovely fresh croissant and *heisse schokolade* (in for a penny, in for a pound, I thought), where I quickly found out how expensive a last-minute one-way flight from Zurich to London could be. Having been semi-unemployed for nine months I wasn't exactly rolling in cash, but I was convinced that if I had called Trafigura and explained the situation, they would have revoked my job offer.

So, after pleading with the less-than-sympathetic airline staff (apparently IOUs are not considered currency at the airport), I forked over my last

$500 and headed back home. Three weeks later I said goodbye to London and said hello to the start of my career in commodity trading.

A few lessons I think can still be applied today are as follows:

- Thoroughly prepare for interviews and, in general, know the job you are going for. However, if you are asked a question you do not know the answer to, do not try to fake it. The people asking the question will tell in an instant that you are not being honest.
- When I graduated, I did not envisage needing to move countries for work, never mind later moving continents. But this industry rewards people who are willing to pursue opportunities wherever they are.
- Switzerland is beautiful but the Swiss German language is not.
- Learn to handle your alcohol.
- If you can afford to wait, do not settle for a job you know you will dislike. I know sometimes that is not an option and you are going to need to generate an income. I was in a privileged position because I could afford to turn down a role at RBS.

Breaking Into the Industry Today

I am frequently contacted by students, graduates, and others with an interest in commodities, all asking the same thing: How can I best position myself to break into commodity trading?

The questions are slightly different, some ask about the best degree, others ask about additional skills that look good on a resume, and others about the best roles to target.

The following advice is based on over fifteen years of direct experience in the industry and on interviewing countless applicants. It is not guaranteed, but it is actionable advice you can follow to increase your chances in what is a highly competitive industry.

<u>You Will Not Be a Trader as a New Graduate</u>

You are not going to get a commercial role out of college. More to the point, you should not want to get a commercial role straight out of college. Too many people try to rush to the front-office with eyes on a big bonus and fail because they do not know enough. Once you are a trader you will be given a very short rope so you want to make sure you are properly qualified before jumping into the role.

So much of commodity trading is learned on the job, so to think that you can jump from a degree to a commercial role is either arrogant or insane.

The Middle-Office is a Perfect Starting Point

Following on from this, if you are serious about a long term career that might end up in a trading role, you should be happy to target entry-level roles. Middle-office (operator, scheduler, etc.) is the best bet because you are so involved in so many aspects of the business. You get exposure (depending on the company) to risk, finance, accounting, credit, and front-office, and you will learn the business from the ground up.

If you cannot get a role in the middle-office you should not be shy about back-office roles. Getting a foot in the door is the most important thing. Once you are in, ask questions of everyone you can without becoming annoying, and be a sponge for information. Finding a mentor in this industry who is willing to take the time and teach you is also worth its weight in gold.

Apply to graduate schemes, but know that the bigger trading houses receive thousands of applications and may offer ten to twenty roles out of each selection process. You should be working at every angle possible - cold and warm contacts, emails, phone calls, and LinkedIn. Use any contact you have in the industry. Ask people if you can buy them a coffee and pick their brain, call companies and ask to speak to someone at the desk about their career. Basically, do whatever you can to build your network and develop connections in the industry.
Work with commodity-specific recruiters. A lot of recruiters are just looking for a quick commission, but some great ones regularly place people at

companies and know what you should have on your resume and where you would be a good fit.

This is a numbers game, and you should be prepared to get ignored often, but you only need one opening.

You should also not only focus on the majors or large trading houses. Small to medium shops can be a great place to learn the business because they typically do not have the number of staff that larger traders do, so your responsibilities might be more than if you were at a larger shop.

Does the Degree Subject Matter?

Your degree is for the most part a means to an end. It is not going to matter whether you have a degree in a science based, math-based, or arts-based subject. Are some subjects looked on more favorably than others? Yes. But it is not the be-all and end-all. Make smart choices about your degree but do not fret over small details.

What you should be more focused on is that you can have a conversation with someone without them feeling like you are smug, arrogant, or a know-it-all. So much of hiring in commodities is based on whether someone wants to sit next to you for nine hours a day without wanting to scream at you. Focus on being likeable and interesting, not the smartest.

You should also be developing a genuine passion for the industry - you do not need to know every nuance, but if you are asked a question in an interview about where the industry might be headed, the interviewer does not want to hear a response that tells them you read a headline and that was it. No one is expecting you to come up with the next best trading idea, but they are expecting you to have an opinion on current trends and the industry as a whole.

Speaking of degrees - masters in commodity trading, is it worth it? This really depends on the program. Some have great professors, and super high placement percentages. Others are frankly not worth the paper the degree is printed on. Do your research, but if I were hiring an employee and had the choice between someone with one to two years of work experience and someone with a master's in commodity trading, I would choose the person with work experience every time.

What Skills Should You Focus On?

In terms of skills you want to be developing, I would be remiss not to talk about coding. It is fast becoming a major asset for any resume and is a plus if you have it. Languages other than English are a huge benefit; the ability to communicate with different cultures is extremely important. Even with advances in translation services, the ability to speak to customers in their mother tongue can drive the relationship.

The most important thing is your soft skills such as communication, emotional intelligence, conflict resolution, and adaptability. This is a relationship-driven industry. If you cannot develop relationships, even in the middle-office, you are not going to have a long career.

You should also be practicing your interview skills. If you are working with a good recruiter they should already be doing mock interviews with you, but get other people to interview you; the stranger they are to you the better. Make yourself uncomfortable so that when you do finally get an interview, you are familiar with the process and not nervous.

What Commodity Should You Target?

At the start of your career you should be completely commodity-agnostic. Almost all the skills you acquire will be transferable across all commodities. Are there nuances to each commodity? Of course. But if you focus on only getting into metals, or oil, or any other commodity, you are drastically narrowing the opportunities available to you. Your primary focus should be to get into any role in a commodities shop, on any commodity. Get grounded in the industry, and if you are good at your job, you will be desirable and you can worry about being specific later in your career.

What Locations Should You Target?

The industry rewards being geographically mobile. This does not mean you will need to switch continents to land a job. But applying to roles outside your current location increases your chances. Plus, if you want a long career in this industry, be prepared to travel a lot.

Good luck to everyone trying to get into this industry; it is a fantastic space to be in, especially right now. There is plenty of opportunity, but it is also highly competitive, so keep plugging away until you find your spot.

Chapter Summary

- You will not begin your career as a trader, nor should you want to. Use early roles to build a solid understanding of the industry before taking on commercial risk.
- The middle-office is the perfect role for new entrants, providing you with exposure to most parts of the business. Back-office roles are also valuable - getting your foot in the door is what matters most.
- Apply through formal schemes but also network relentlessly. Use LinkedIn, phone calls, and coffee chats to speak to people in the industry.
- Don't fixate on one commodity or geography - skills are transferable and mobility often increases opportunity.
- There is no single 'correct' degree for commodity trading. Hiring comes down to personality far more than education.
- Coding and digital literacy are increasingly required but soft skills like communication and adaptability remain your biggest edge.
- Practice interviews until you can communicate confidently, listen actively, and hold a genuine conversation.
- Breaking in is a numbers game. You will face rejection and silence, but you only need one opportunity to change everything.

My Origin Story

Commodities are in my blood.

With a surname like Basi, I often get asked about my family's origin. When I tell people that I am half English and half Indian, it usually surprises them - primarily because of my ambiguous skin tone and strong South East London accent.

There was even a sizable bet at the Trafigura India office about whether I was *really* Indian. To settle it, I had to reveal the name of the village my dad grew up in - Bundala, in Punjab (for those curious).

As part of my grandparents' sixtieth wedding anniversary, my dad created a family tree that traced our roots back 500 years. The Basi family actually began with two Italian brothers - merchants involved in the spice trade between Italy and India. On one of their voyages, they decided to stay in India. Back then, the name was spelled *Bassi*, but they dropped an "s", and eventually, Basi became a village name.

500 years later, I found myself embarking on my own commodities voyage - one that also spanned oceans, though thankfully by airplane, not sailboat.

It's funny how history repeats itself. From spice traders to metals traders, the Basi journey continues.

19. Glossary

Arbitrage: The buying and selling of a commodity to exploit price differences in two different markets for that same commodity.

Assaying: The laboratory analysis of commodities to determine the precise chemical composition.

Benchmark price: A widely recognized pricing reference, often published by an exchange or price reporting agency, used as the basis for pricing physical trades.

Bilateral finance line: A one-to-one lending agreement between a trader and a single lender.

Bill of lading (BOL/BL): A legal title document issued by a carrier that serves as proof of ownership for goods in transit.

Blending: The process of combining different grades or qualities of a commodity to achieve a desired specification or to optimize value.

Bonded storage: A facility authorized by local customs authorities where goods may be stored without payment of duties until they enter the domestic market.

Borrowing base: A secured financing structure where the lender advances funds based on the value of pledged collateral, typically inventory or receivables.

Bulk vessel: Standard vessel classes defined by their deadweight tonnage (DWT) and operational limitations.

Cash financing: Payment for commodities using a company's own equity rather than bank credit lines.

Charterer: A party that hires a vessel for a voyage or period of time to transport cargo.

Collateral: Assets pledged to secure a loan.

Commodity: A standardized, largely interchangeable raw material that can be traded globally. Unlike finished consumer goods, commodities share defined specifications that make them broadly fungible.

Conditional release: A document issued by a storage facility confirming goods will be released once specified payment conditions are met.

Concentrates/ores: Partially processed or raw mined materials containing valuable metals, typically requiring further refining.

Customs clearance: The process of obtaining government approval for export or import of goods.

Deadweight tonnage (DWT): The maximum weight a vessel can safely carry including cargo, fuel, provisions, and crew.

Demurrage: A financial penalty paid by charterers or cargo owners when loading or unloading a vessel exceeds the agreed time allowed.

Detention: Charges are applied when containers or equipment are held beyond the free time allowed outside the terminal.

Dispatch: A rebate paid by the vessel owner to the charterer for using less laytime than allowed.

Environmental, social, and governance (ESG): The framework used to evaluate a company's performance and responsible conduct across three pillars: How a company affects the natural environment; how a company manages relationships with its employees and local communities; and the leadership structures that guide corporate behavior.

Exchange-approved storage: A warehouse, tank, or facility authorized by an exchange to hold deliverable inventory meeting exchange-set standards.

Exposure: The financial or operations risk a company faces because of open positions.

Factoring: Selling receivables to a third party for early repayment, either with or without recourse.

Force majeure: A contractual clause relieving parties of liability when extraordinary events prevent performance.

Freight forwarder: A logistics service provider that arranges transportation and documentation for cargo movement.

Futures contract: A standardized agreement traded on an exchange to buy or sell a commodity at a future date.

Futures exchange: A regulated marketplace where futures contracts are traded.

Full release: A document instructing a storage facility to transfer control of goods to a named party.

Fundamental analysis: Determining the physical supply and demand of a commodity in the market. Can be performed on a local, regional, or global level.

Grade (commodity grade): A defined quality or specification standard for a commodity.

Haircut: The percentage reduction a lender applies to the value of collateral to mitigate price risk.

Hard commodity: Natural resources that are extracted or mined, such as crude oil, natural gas, coal, iron ore, copper, aluminum, gold and silver, and can be stored for long periods of time without degradation.

Hedged repo: A financing structure in which the lender received both title to inventory and a matching futures hedge.

Hedging: Using futures or other derivatives to offset price risk in physical contracts.

Holding certificate (HC): A document confirming inventory held at a location. Not usually recognized as a title document unless contractually agreed.

Incoterms: Internationally standardized trade terms defining logistics responsibilities, cost allocation, and risk transfer.

Inspection certificate: A document issued by an independent surveyor confirming the quality, quantity, or condition of goods.

KYC (know your counterparty): Due diligence on counterparties to assess creditworthiness, compliance risk, and reputation, carried out before engaging in trading activities.

Laycan: The agreed window during which a vessel must arrive for loading.

LC (letter of credit): A bank guarantee ensuring payment to a seller once specified documentation is presented.

Logistics: The movement of goods from origin to destination including transport, storage, documentation and handling.

Margin call: A demand by a clearing house or broker for additional funds to cover mark-to-market losses.

Margin (initial and variation): Collateral required to open and maintain a futures trade.

Mark-to-market (MTM): A form of accounting that allows businesses to recognize unrealized gains or losses at the inception of a deal.
Market liquidity: The ease with which a commodity or derivative instrument can be traded without significantly affecting the price.

Metric ton (mt): A unit equal to 1,000 kilograms, commonly used in commodity trading.

Moisture: The level of water content contained in a commodity.

Non-exchange storage: Storage facilities not approved by exchanges, often offering lower costs but requiring greater due diligence.

Notify party: The entity listed on a bill of lading to be notified upon vessel arrival.

On board date: The date goods are confirmed to be loaded onto a vessel.

Operational risk: Risk arising from logistics disruptions, infrastructure failure, or human error.

Payment terms (net 30, net 60, etc.): Contractual payment timelines following receipt of goods or the invoice.

Pipeline ticket: A document evidencing the volume of a liquid commodity transferred via pipeline and held in a party's name.

Premium/discount: The value added or deducted from a benchmark price based on quality, logistics, or contractual terms.

Profit and loss (P&L): The gross amount a trader gains or loses on a trade.

Provisional release: A preliminary confirmation from a warehouse indicating goods are ready for release but not yet transferred.

QP (quotational period): The pricing window during which the final price of a commodity is determined.

Quality claim: A dispute arises when delivered material fails to meet contractual quality specifications.

Repo: A financing transaction where a trader sells goods to a lender and agrees to repurchase them later at a set price.

Revolving credit facility (RCF): A loan that allows a borrower to draw, repay, and redraw funds up to a specific amount during the term of a loan. The trader does not have to ask the lender to approve each transaction.

Sampling: The extraction of representative material to assess quality and composition.

Soft commodity: Resources that are grown such as agricultural products including wheat, corn, coffee, cotton, soybeans, cattle, and hogs; and are more sensitive to seasonality, weather, disease, and spoilage.

Structured finance: Non-traditional financing methods including bonds, and inventory-backed structures.

Surveyor: An independent third party hired to verify weight, quality, quantity, or condition.

SWIFT confirmation: A secure financial message confirming that payment has been initiated.

Tare weight: The weight of empty containers or transport equipment.

Tank receipt: A title document representing ownership of fungible liquid commodities stored in a tank.

Terminal handling charges (THC): Fees charged by ports for loading and unloading containers.

Title document: A legally recognized document such as a bill of lading or warehouse receipt, establishing ownership of goods.

Trade finance: Financing structures used to support the movement and sale of physical commodities.

Verified gross mass (VGM): The certified weight of a loaded container, required before it can be loaded onto a vessel.

Volatility: A measure of price fluctuation in a market over time.

Warehouse receipt: A title document issued by a warehouse confirming ownership of stored goods.

Weighing: The process of determining the exact quantity of a commodity for invoicing and settlement.

Working capital: The liquidity required to finance day-to-day trading activities.

WSMD (Weighing, Sampling, Moisture Determination and Assaying): The four core processes used to determine the quality and quantity of commodity deliveries.

PERFECTLY HEDGED

Interested in learning more?
In-person and online training available.
Visit our website for additional information.

Join the Perfectly Hedged community!
Follow us on LinkedIn for new insights,
updates and exclusive offers.

Let's connect, I'd love to hear from you:

SAMUEL BASI
Founder & Author
Perfectly Hedged LLC

+1 203-391-8021
samuel.basi@perfectlyhedged.com
www.perfectlyhedged.com
linkedin.com/company/perfectly-hedged-llc

www.ingramcontent.com/pod-product-compliance
Lightning Source LLC
LaVergne TN
LVHW100308210926
848480LV00003B/1063
9798295669712